OXFORD WORLD'S CLASSICS

ANTIGONE

AND OTHER TRAGEDIES

SOPHOCLES, who died in 405 BC at the age of about 90, was a prominent citizen of Athens during what was in many ways her Golden Age. Fifth-century democratic Athens became the coordinator and eventually imperial head of a powerful naval confederacy, and enjoyed an era of extraordinary prosperity and cultural activity. In his time Sophocles was a Military Commander, a Confederacy Treasurer, and a Special Executive after the disastrous expedition to Sicily in 415–3. He was legendary for his easygoing character, conviviality and energetic sex-life. His lifetime saw the growth of what we know as History and Philosophy; it also turned the recently developed genre of Tragedy into a major art-form of poetry and performance which has stood the test of time for two-and-a-half millennia.

Sophocles composed and produced more than 120 plays, competing in the annual dramatic competitions on average every other year throughout his long adult life. For some twelve years he overlapped with the older Aeschylus and for nearly fifty with the slightly younger Euripides; he won the first prize more often than either of them. Only seven of his tragedies survive, and we can securely date only two: *Philoctetes* and *Oedipus at Colonus* both come from the last years of his life. Already in his own lifetime Sophocles' two most famous plays seem to have been *Antigone and Oedipus the King*: the former probably dates from the first third of his career and the latter from the middle third.

Sophocles' tragedies engage with fundamental problems and issues of human life while also moving the deepest and darkest emotions in their audience. Few figures in world literature have exerted such lasting and varied influence.

OLIVER TAPLIN is Emeritus Professor of Classics at the University of Oxford. His work focuses on the reception of poetry and drama through performance and material culture in both ancient and modern times.

OXFORD WORLD'S CLASSICS

For over 100 years Oxford World's Classics have brought readers closer to the world's great literature. Now with over 700 titles—from the 4,000-year-old myths of Mesopotamia to the twentieth century's greatest novels—the series makes available lesser-known as well as celebrated writing.

The pocket-sized hardbacks of the early years contained introductions by Virginia Woolf, T. S. Eliot, Graham Greene, and other literary figures which enriched the experience of reading. Today the series is recognized for its fine scholarship and reliability in texts that span world literature, drama and poetry, religion, philosophy, and politics. Each edition includes perceptive commentary and essential background information to meet the changing needs of readers.

OXFORD WORLD'S CLASSICS

SOPHOCLES

Antigone • Deianeira • Electra

Translated with an Introduction and Notes by

OLIVER TAPLIN

UNIVERSITY PRESS

Great Clarendon Street, Oxford, OX2 6DP,
United Kingdom

Oxford University Press is a department of the University of Oxford.
It furthers the University's objective of excellence in research, scholarship,
and education by publishing worldwide. Oxford is a registered trade mark of
Oxford University Press in the UK and in certain other countries

First published 2020, as *Sophocles: Antigone and other Tragedies*
First published as an Oxford World's Classics paperback 2021

Impression: 1

Published in the United States of America by Oxford University Press
198 Madison Avenue, New York, NY 10016, United States of America

British Library Cataloguing in Publication Data
Data available

Library of Congress Control Number: 2021943242

ISBN 978–0–19–280686–4

Printed and bound in Great Britain by
Clays Ltd, Elcograf S.p.A.

For
Peter and Kitty
George and Jim

FOREWORD

The first volume of my translations of Sophocles, published in 2015, collected what I think of as his four 'male' tragedies. This one contains the three 'female' tragedies, each named after their key character (which has called for the change of the traditional title *Women of Trachis* to *Deianeira*). I first conceived the ambition of translating Sophocles into verse as a student when I embarked on Antigone (inevitably!). At that time, more than 50 years ago, this kind of version would probably have been regarded as rather 'free': these days it might seem relatively 'close'. In any case, something that I hope distinguishes it from most other translations of whatever kind of relationship to Sophocles is the attempt to infuse some inherent musicality and colour into the language, especially (but not only) in the lyric passages. To realize how this works I urge readers to sound it out aloud, or even better perform it in a group. Best of all would be to stage it with music.

I have much to be grateful for, and there are some people I would especially like to thank. These include Karen Raith, Henry Clarke, Lisa Eaton, and Peter Gibbs for their roles in the production of the book for the Press. I take the opportunity to acknowledge four friends who are also exemplars of scholarship to emulate: Pat Easterling, Fiona Macintosh, Peter Wilson, and Felix Budelmann. At home, Charis has been an ever-changing source of fresh ideas, and Beaty has been a constant encourager and a sensitive sounding-board. The dedication names friends who have remained close even though on the other side of the globe.

O.T.

At the time of coronavirus

CONTENTS

INTRODUCTION: SOPHOCLES AND HIS THEATRE

Sophocles and Tragedy

SOPHOCLES tends to get cast as the 'good boy' of classical Greek tragedy, by contrast with Aeschylus and Euripides. Characterizations (or caricatures) of the 'great three'[1] are already being set up in Aristophanes' fantastical comedy *Frogs*, first put on in 405 BC,[2] soon after the death of Euripides, and even sooner after that of Sophocles. Aeschylus is the rugged pioneer, heavy-handed, grandiloquent, advocating old-fashioned values; Euripides is clever, subversive, proletarian, undermining traditional norms; Sophocles is just a good chap, 'genial up here above, and genial down there below' (*Frogs* line 82). The infusion of this portrait into colouring the perception of his entire work is epitomized by Matthew Arnold in the mid-nineteenth century, when he thanks Sophocles and his 'even-balanced soul':

> Who saw life steadily, and saw it whole;
> The mellow glory of the Attic stage. . . .

Yet I, for one, do not find this view confirmed by the plays themselves. Far from it. A couple of choral odes affirming traditional religion and the Justice of Zeus do not make the tragedies serene or balanced or freighted with grave wisdom. Sophocles' plays are deeply disturbing and unpredictable, unrelenting and open-ended, constantly refusing to stand firm on any consistent good-versus-bad situations or any redemptive justification of the ways of gods to men—or women. Arnold caught his vision of life far more perceptively when he wrote of Sophocles reflecting 'the turbid ebb and flow of human misery'.[3] At the same time it is undeniable that what we know of Sophocles the man consistently portrays him as a sociable, prosperous citizen, not at

[1] All of the tragedies (out of many hundreds) that survive today are by these three except for two 'anon.': *Prometheus*, which comes down under the name of Aeschylus, and *Rhesus*, under the name of Euripides.

[2] All dates BC unless otherwise specified.

[3] In his famous poem 'Dover Beach'. I cannot resist noting, though, that Arnold was wrong to suppose that Sophocles heard the same sound of the ebb and flow as he heard at Dover: the waves in the Aegean break significantly more frequently.

all the tortured soul we might expect (or even wish for?). But it is simplistic ideas about the relationship between creative artists and their work that should be adjusted.

What then, in the end, is particular about Sophocles' kind of tragedy? Is there something distinctively Sophoclean in his world-view, his 'philosophy', his whole burden? Some of the ways which have been standardly claimed as uniquely Sophoclean do not really stand up to scrutiny. There seems, above all, to have been a desire for him to conform to some model of steadiness or solidity (as in the Matthew Arnold). But the plays themselves are constantly unbalancing this claim with leaps and twists, both of plot and of ethical weighting. The turbid suffering of the human world is—so far as I can see, at least—no more measured or just or explicable in Sophocles' plays than in any other great tragic literature. Nor are his plays, as has often been claimed, distinctly conservative, or especially pious.[4] There is rather more truth to the branding of Sophocles as a 'pessimist'. Tragedy may not be the obvious resource to go for optimism in the first place! Nonetheless it may be true that Sophocles tends to offer less counterbalancing relief or consolation than most tragic drama. At the same time his plays do not lead towards unqualified despair or resignation: on the contrary they are in their own way strengthening.

What makes Sophocles special is not so much a 'message' or 'philosophy', but an intense vision of the human world amidst its pain. It is not a matter of world-view so much as of atmospheric clarity, like on one of those days when you can see every detail of far-distant hills. That is to say that Sophocles' plays do what tragedy characteristically does, and with singularly stark focus. What I mean by 'What tragedy characteristically does' is this (to put it very simply and very briefly): to set up a complex and inextricable combination of strong emotion and challenging thought across a range of human experience in order to reach towards making some kind of sense out of human suffering. The fusion of emotion and cognitive engagement produce form, perceptible shape expressed in movement, poetry, and music.

The emotions aroused in Greek tragedy, and Sophocles in particular, go far beyond the cliché formulation of 'pity and fear'—although

[4] As E. M. Forster has an enlightened teacher put it in *The Longest Journey*, 'Boys will regard Sophocles as a kind of enlightened bishop, and something tells me that they are wrong.'

pity is certainly central. Any full account would have to include grief, horror, indignation, disgust, affection, excitement, joy, elation, anguish, helplessness—all of them felt in anticipation and in the present and in retrospect.[5]

As for the range of issues on which Sophoclean tragedy provoked thought, an abbreviated list can do no more than to suggest their complexity and breadth. There are politics—in the sense of living in societies—power, persuasion, war, justice, revenge. There are the family, its bonds and conflicts, blood-kin, marriage, bereavement. There are the conflicts and interactions of male and female, public and interior, power and weakness, love and hate, hurtfulness and protectiveness. Emotions and their causes are thought about as well as felt—their rationality and irrationality, their justification and their harmfulness. Add to all that the workings of the mind, madness, how far motives are conscious, the benefits and dangers of rationality; responsibility, free will, determinism, the extent of choice, the attribution of blame. Tragedy further confronts the nature of truth, relativity, existence and seeming. And, not least, there are the gods—or the human sense of superhuman powers—whether the transcendent is malign or benign; whether the divine has any sense of justice; whether it can be understood, or is essentially incomprehensible. This amounts, all in all, to a panorama that takes in nothing less than the meaning or meaninglessness of life, of grief, of death.

The best proof of these large claims—the eating of the pudding, so to speak—lies not in my lumbering formulations, but in the huge variety of inspirations and provocations that have been brought to fruition by later ages in response to Sophocles' seven surviving plays. Since there is no way of doing justice to any particular instances in this context, the point may be made by scattering a spread of names from the last few generations, without specifying their very varied, and even contradictory, responses. Think of G. F. Hegel, Sigmund Freud, Judith Butler; think of Friedrich Hölderlin, W. B. Yeats, Ezra Pound, Seamus Heaney, Anne Carson; Thomas Hardy, Hugo von Hofmannstal, Jean Anouilh, Bert Brecht, Athol Fugard, Heiner Müller, Rita Dove; bear in mind Felix Mendelssohn, Max Reinhardt, Igor Stravinsky, Martha Graham, Pier Paolo Pasolini, Luis Alfaro. . . . The point is

[5] I am deliberately avoiding the technical term 'catharsis', made central by Aristotle, because it is not as clear or as self-evident as it is often taken to be.

that Sophocles has meant so much and so many different things to such different creative artists and thinkers, and in so many art-forms. He has offered them handles, threads, shapes to hold on to.

If I have, then, to try to pick out two characteristics of Sophocles that have imparted to his plays such staying power and such adaptability, it would be these. First, there is the brave, unflinching facing up to suffering, the engagement with 'the human condition' in all its darker and more heart-rending aspects. No blinking, no evasion, no palliative. The creative form emerges with such focus because there is no blurring or sideways glancing or postponement.

Secondly, in the face of this sombre fixity, Sophocles' plays are, nonetheless, never reduced to inarticulacy or chaos or despair. They remain strong and engaged even amid the turbid ebb and flow; they find poetry and lyric and heat and light even in the most arctic and tempestuous conditions of human life. The most terrible possibilities are exposed and faced, and yet the response becomes crafted words and movements and song. The tragedies 'face the music', and they do that by turning it into poetry and music. The sorrows are thus transmuted into a kind of benefit, and even beauty. Out of apparently meaningless suffering comes meaning and form. And so the spectator or reader is strengthened and extended for pressing on through the experience of life.

Sophocles in his Time and Place

It so happens that Sophocles' long life coincided almost exactly with the years of the great 'golden' age of Greek tragic theatre; and that very nearly synchronizes with the period that our calendar calibrates as the 'fifth century BC'. Aeschylus is said to have put on his first production in 499, and it is clear that he and his contemporaries were already producing fully fledged and serious tragedies in the 490s, the decade during which Sophocles was born. It is a plausible view that tragedy had suddenly burst on the cultural and poetic scene at Athens not long before then; and, if so, this would mean that the whole enterprise of Theatre and of Tragedy was born only some ten or twenty years before Sophocles himself.[6]

[6] We know next to nothing for sure about the origin of theatre and of tragedy, but it is much more likely, in my opinion, to have been a sudden, inspired innovation than the product of a long and gradual development from primitive rituals. But this is, of course, a much-disputed subject.

Sophocles first put on tragedies in 468 (and won first prize at first attempt, it is said). For the first dozen years of his career he was competing with the great Aeschylus at the height of his powers; for the next fifty years after that his chief rival was Euripides, who was some fifteen years younger. It would be a condescending mistake to suppose that all the other playwrights of the time were inferior second-raters, but, as *Frogs* shows, these two were recognized in their own day as the greatest creative poets and dramatists of the age.

This was the very period which saw Athens pass through its greatest cultural and economic flowering. The city then went on to confront the toils of disease and war, although since both Euripides and Sophocles died within a few months of each other in 407–6, they did not live to see the war end with the humiliating defeat of Athens by Sparta and her allies in 404.[7] The years of Sophocles' maturity, say between about 460 and 432, were the heady, and relatively peaceful, years when Athens produced one of the most creative cultures ever known in human history. With an allowance of simplification, one might say that History and Philosophy were both invented in this very time and place; the Parthenon was built; many of the finest artworks of ancient Greece radiated from this cultural hub. This one city—the largest in the Greek world at the time, with a population of male citizens of about 30,000—housed, among others, Socrates, Phidias, Protagoras, Pericles, and Herodotus (a personal friend of Sophocles). And the next generation, that growing up in Sophocles' later years, included Plato, Thucydides, and Aristophanes.

Within this prolific era Sophocles emerges as a central and congenial figure—rich, attractive, sociable—and a great poet. Anecdotes clustered around his exploits, especially his love-life and his table-talk, but he did also participate in the public life of the city. One year he was an official Treasurer; in another (possibly more than once) he was one of the ten elected military Commanders; and late in life in 413 he was one of the ten 'Councilors' convened after Athens had suffered military disaster in Sicily. A genial spirit, then, a famous lover (of both sexes), a good citizen, a model public figure. All this

[7] This was, however, very far from the end of Athens, as it is often portrayed. Nor was it the Death of Tragedy (despite Nietzsche, among others). There was at least another century of creative activity in the theatre; but it was a 'silver age' compared with the fifth century—and all too little survives from it.

might not fit our preconceptions of the kind of person who should produce disconcerting, soul-scouring tragedies. But, just as it took Athens at the crest of its strength and prosperity to create the whole genre of tragedy, it arguably took a person of confidence and security to drive its portrayal of life so far into the dark terrains of the human condition without flinching. It is as though he takes his audience to the verge of the abyss, and then keeps his feet so firmly planted in the stuff of human resilience that he can then hold them back from falling into the black hole, returning them unharmed, and even strengthened, to everyday life.

Such fierce material needed a kind of heat-proof crucible to contain it. It could only dare to become so harrowing and challenging once the surrounding society in Athens had set up an occasion to hold it without danger of corrosion. Whether the genesis of tragedy was long and gradual or a sudden invention (as I believe), its stature as a major art-form was undoubtedly indivisible from the inauguration of a major festival as the occasion for performances. And it is surely no coincidence that this was founded, or at least became centrally important, at just the same time as the first establishment of a democratic constitution in 508, a revolution which, to an unprecedented extent, handed over power to the whole people (*demos*). This festival, the Great Dionysia (also known as the City Dionysia) was open for all citizens to attend; it was held every spring in a sloping area sacred to the god Dionysus beneath the Acropolis. There was room here for several thousands of spectators to gather and witness the pre-rehearsed actors and chorus. It was probably the first festival in ancient Greece to be devoted exclusively to poetry, without any admixture of athletics and other such events. There were also smaller Dionysia held in villages throughout Attica; and serious theatrical performances, far from rudimentary or rustic, were put on at these as well.

All of Sophocles' plays were, so far as we know, created for first performance at the Great Dionysia. Right from the beginning it seems that they were organized according to much the same programme as they continued to have during Sophocles' time.[8] A first day was given over to dithyrambs, a pre-dramatic form of choral poetry; and then three days were devoted to tragedy, with one tragedian putting on his

[8] Comedy was added to the bill in the 480s. It does not seem, however, to have made its impact as a considerable art-form before the 440s or 430s.

work each day. This took the form of three tragedies followed by a satyr-play, all performed by the same team of actors and chorus.[9] These were, as with so many occasions in ancient Greece, mounted as a competition. Quite highly organized conventions controlled the recruitment, financing, and status of the fifteen members of the chorus, who had to be Athenian citizens (they may have been twelve in early days). In Sophocles' time there were three male actors (not necessarily Athenian), but in earlier times there had been only two. These took on all the individual roles between them, changing mask and costume as needed. The playwright himself was known as the *didaskalos*, the teacher, presumably because of his role in the development and rehearsal of the production.

The evidence seems firm that Sophocles composed between 120 and 130 plays over his long career. Supposing that these were all in sets of four for the Great Dionysia, he will have put on plays for some thirty-one annual festivals, in other words for about half of all those held over the course of his adult life. It is recorded that he won first prize on well over half of these occasions. Yet, of these many plays only seven tragedies have come down to us, and no complete satyr-plays.[10] Most of his works evidently survived intact until about AD 200 or 300, but after that only the seven which we have continued to be much copied. They were selected for primarily educational purposes. *Oedipus the King* and *Antigone* were always his most famous plays; and they presumably account for the selection of *Oedipus at Colonus* as a kind of companion piece. It should be emphasized, though, that these three plays were not originally conceived of as a trilogy, nor performed as one. *Aias* and *Electra* were also widely read and performed from early days. We cannot really say, however, why the other two, *Deianeira*[11] and *Philoctetes* were selected.

[9] Satyr-plays, where the chorus always took on the role of satyrs, those scandalously undisciplined followers of Dionysus, may have been introduced later than tragedy, but soon became a core component. The plays were set in the world of tragic myth, but outside the bounds of society and order, often entertainingly exploring origins for institutions of the human world.

[10] We have hundreds of fragments from the lost plays, but few are more than a line or two long. It so happens that the largest fragments by far, preserved on a papyrus, contain about half of a satyr-play, *Satyrs on the Track* (*Ichneutai*).

[11] This is the title adopted in this translation for the play originally titled *Trachiniai* (*Women of Trachis*). For justification of this change see p. 67.

Scholars have not got very far with placing the seven surviving plays chronologically within Athenian history and Sophocles' career. The only two with firm dates are from near the end: *Philoctetes* was first put on in 409, and *Oedipus at Colonus* only after his death. There are anecdotes which date *Antigone* to 442, but, while that date is not in itself implausible, the stories are probably fictional. Otherwise, internal evidence of style and technique offer little help, except to indicate that *Electra* was relatively late, probably after 420. It is quite likely that *Deianeira*, *Antigone*, and *Aias* were all first produced somewhere between 455 and 435, but this is far from sure; and scholarly studies suggest, though not firmly, that *Oedipus the King* was later than these other three plays, most likely dating from the 430s or 420s.

Biographers like to detect a progression in an artist's oeuvre, and tend to order works in a sequence from juvenilia to high maturity to 'last things'. But, apart from the two late works, which would have been probably dateable even without the external evidence, Sophocles generally denies us such progressions, whether naïve or sophisticated. So the three plays in this volume are not related by chronology or mind-set: in fact the main feature which they have in common is a central female character. In *Deianeira* and *Antigone* she is alive for only the first two-thirds of the play, but in both is clearly the most interesting character. Both Deianeira and Electra have the support of a sympathetic female chorus, but Antigone is more isolated with a chorus of Thebes elders. This division of Sophocles' seven surviving plays between the two volumes is thus entirely editorial; but it does, at least, have more of a significant connection through gender than the standard gathering of so-called 'Theban plays'.

Myth and Innovation

One notion that sustains the fallacious image of Sophocles as some kind of rock-like monument (however 'mellow') is that his plots are driven by the inexorable will of the gods or by Fate. The audience knows the story already, this account goes, and helplessly watches them enact their predetermined doom, however much they may struggle against it. As the Prologue of Cocteau's Oedipus play puts it, 'Before you is a fully wound machine. Slowly its spring will unwind the entire span of a human life. It is one of the most perfect machines devised by the infernal gods for the mathematical annihilation of a mortal.'[12] But on the human level Sophocles' characters clearly determine their own fate; they are in no way mere pawns or puppets. And, in any case, the audience did not know the whole story already. This becomes clear if one takes a step back and looks at Tragedy as story-telling.

The fundamental revolution brought about by the invention of theatre in Athens was that the stories were told through enactment and embodiment without any narrative framing. The scene before the spectators became the world of the story, the actors became the agents, the chorus became participants integrated into that world. We take it for granted that the stories told in Greek tragedies were set back in the great 'heroic' age, the world that had already supplied epic poems for hundreds of years before. But when the Athenians first developed their new dramatic art-form, that would not have been the only possibility; they might, for example, have told stories of gods, or narratives drawn from more recent historical times.[13] Yet, from its earliest stages tragedy settled on the old myths.

This seems to have been, in effect, a master-stroke of prescience, a kind of intuition that these would hold almost limitless potential for future development. This capacity is partly thanks to their combination of the immediate and the remote, so that the plots contain dynamic combinations of high nobility with family strife, of distance in social and political terms, yet topicality of places, cults, and institutions. But another important factor was surely that, if the new art-form was to set itself up as a serious rival to the traditional genres of epic and large-scale choral poetry, it was going to have to challenge them on their own ground. Tragedy's claim was to provide everything that they could offer plus the whole new and unmatchably vivid dimension of direct enactment. It even followed and capped epic poetry by taking on its two core story-clusters, namely the events of the Trojan War and its aftermath, and the dynastic struggles at Thebes.[14]

[12] *La Machine Infernale*, first performed in 1934.

[13] Aeschylus' *Persians* of 472 is an example of this, but historical tragedy never became mainstream. Plays about Prometheus are the only known example of tragedies telling of immortals rather than humans.

[14] Hesiod (early seventh century) says the Age of Bronze inhabited by 'demigod-heroes' was wiped out by these two great wars. A key turning-point in tragedy's challenge to epic must have been Aeschylus' *Achilles*-trilogy (probably from the 490s), which refashioned the main plot-sequence of the *Iliad* into three plays.

The tragic versions of these mythical narratives had another enormous advantage over epic and lyric versions, one that undoubtedly helped to eclipse them: the potential for change and innovation. The epic poems, especially the *Iliad* and *Odyssey*, were frequently performed in the fifth century, but the words ('text' is a rather anachronistic term) were more or less fixed. Indeed an agreed wording might have been indispensable for the coordination of competitions held between the performers of epic, the rhapsodes. But Tragedy did not have any call to stick closely to previous versions: on the contrary, part of the excitement of the competition lay in finding new ways of manipulating the old stories. Variations, changes, and innovations were positively welcome, provided that they were persuasive and purposeful.

So tragedy was constantly making use of earlier versions, but in order to depart from them as much as to follow them. Both Aeschylus and Euripides had, for example, previously dramatized the fetching of Philoctetes to Troy from Lemnos, but, while both had employed several more characters than Sophocles, neither of them introduced Neoptolemus. This is Sophocles' innovation and it radically changes the whole dynamic of the play. The most extreme example of innovation in surviving Sophocles is *Antigone*. While he may not have actually invented Antigone herself, it is very probable that the whole story of her going to her death in order to bury her brother was his own creation (see further p. 3). Jean Anouilh[15] has his Prologue-figure say that, much as this young woman would have liked to live, 'there's nothing to be done. Her name is Antigone, and she must play her part through to the end'. But the real reason why Antigone must play her part is because Sophocles created that part.

So it was integral to the whole strength of tragedy that each play was *not* predictable, neither in its dramatic structure nor in detail of plot. The genre encouraged novelty, though nearly always deployed within the basic conventions of the art-form. So the familiar dogma that 'they all knew the story already' is quite simply false: they never know what unforeseeable turns the dramatization was going to take. In keeping with this, the myths, while traditional in many ways, did not incorporate any sort of inexorability or 'Fate' intrinsically built into

[15] First performed in Paris in February 1944. It was passed by the occupying German censors, even though seen by some as a gesture of resistance.

them. Sophocles was no less inventive in both narrative and in dramatic technique than Euripides and his other rivals.

The Sights of Greek Tragedy

When we talk about the birth or invention of Tragedy—which means in effect the invention of Theatre—we tend to think above all about myths, themes, issues, world-views. But there had to be a crucial physical and performative dimension to all this as well. There had to be the 'personnel' in the first place: the actors, chorus, playwright, musician, stage managers, financiers, etc., who all collaborated in advance to prepare and rehearse the works. And there had to be a coordinated audience who knew both the time (the festival of Dionysus) and the place where they should gather in a *theatron*—which means 'viewing-place'—in order to see the work performed. Until all that had been set up there was no theatre in any relevant sense, and so no Tragedy.

Ancient Greek theatres were invariably huge open-air viewing-places with room for thousands, rather than hundreds, of spectators. The actual performance-space was a large, flat area at the foot of a slope and/or raked seating ('bleachers' is the useful American term). All of Sophocles' plays were, so far as we know, composed for the *theatron* in the area sacred to Dionysus at Athens, which made use of the slope beneath the south-east segment of the Acropolis.

It used to be regarded as beyond question that the performance space, the *orchestra* (literally 'dance-place') was circular; and that did, indeed, become the standard form for theatres in the fourth century, such as the most famous example at Epidaurus. Many scholars now believe, however, that back in the fifth century the *orchestra* was rectangular, on the grounds that the stone seating at the front was built in an arc of straight segments. But since most of the seating in Sophocles' day was constructed in wood, it is not unexpected that the stone seating should be in similarly straight stretches. That is, in fact, still compatible with a circular *orchestra*; and I am personally inclined to favour the circle as providing both a more unified viewing-focus and a better dance-space. It also used to be generally accepted that the audience-slope in Sophocles' day was large enough to seat some 12,000–15,000, a figure reached (again) by extrapolating from fourth-century auditoria. It now transpires that in the fifth century there were some houses half way up the slope, which might indicate an audience of 'only' about 6,000 (still a huge number of people!). It is, however, not out of the question that some of the audience sat around and above the house-plots.

Whatever the truth of these disputed issues, the basic lay-out of the performance space, as it is incorporated into the fabric of the plays, is pretty clear and relatively uncontroversial. On the far side of the *orchestra* was the stage-building, the *skene*, with a wide central door.[16] This most often represented some kind of house or palace. In both *Antigone* and *Electra* this is the ancestral royal palace, the seat of power, however contested; in *Deianeira* it is the house where the family of Heracles has settled in Trachis. Both actors and chorus shared the *orchestra*-space without special differentiation. It may well be, however, that the actors tended to perform in the section further away from the audience. It is possible there was a low stage-platform in front of the *skene* at Athens, but there is no clear indication of this in any of our plays.[17]

Scene-painting was being developed in the time of Sophocles, and was especially associated with techniques for representing perspective. It is not known, however, whether the same panels of scene-painting remained in place throughout each year's festival, or whether they were changed for each playwright, or, indeed, for each play. The variety of settings that we find in the plays could obviously make use of specific scene-painting that changed for each one, if it was available. But, even without any play-specific painting, the signification of the location and background are clearly established within each play.

There were also two pieces of theatrical machinery, which, to judge from allusions in contemporary comedy, were particularly associated with tragic theatre. One, the *ekkyklema* (the 'roll-out'), was a wheeled platform which could be extruded from the central door: its core function was to make internal scenes visible on stage. Within the three plays in this volume, it is possible that it was employed to reveal the body of Eurydice in *Antigone* (see note on 1293); and it was undoubtedly used in *Electra* to reveal the tableau of the body of Clytemnestra

[16] The *skene* is very important for Aeschylus' *Oresteia* of 458 BC, but it is not agreed whether or not it existed before then.

[17] We know from comic vase-paintings that in the theatres of the Greek West (south Italy and Sicily) there was standardly a wooden stage-platform of about 1 metre high, with steps going up to it. This feature is already there in the earliest paintings from about 400 BC.

with Orestes and Pylades standing by (see note on 1463). The other, the *mechane* (the 'device'), was some kind of crane used to carry actors through the air, especially those playing gods, so that they are to be imagined as flying. This is especially associated with divine epiphanies at the end of Euripides' tragedies; these are the so-called *theos apo mechanes* or *deus ex machina*.

To either side of the acting-area were entrance-ways, in effect roads that were visible to the audience for at least several metres (known as *eisodoi* or *parodoi*). These did not have a rigidly fixed signification; but a clear sense of 'topography' is still established internally within each play. Often these two directions were dramatically important, usually in opposition to each other; and Sophocles paid particular attention to this spatial dimension. The significance of the two directions in the three tragedies in this volume are set out in the notice at the beginning of each play.

It is questionable whether there were any fixed structures within the *orchestra*. It is conventionally supposed that there was an altar of Dionysus, but this is far from certain. What is certain is that some plays, for example the opening scenes of *Oedipus the King*, call for a stage altar; but that was more probably a portable painted prop; it also looks likely that in *Electra* there was a stage-statue of Apollo in front of the palace. Portable furniture such as thrones, couches, etc., were available when called for, and, like all the props and masks, these were the responsibility of the *skeuopoios*, the 'equipment-maker'.

The actors and chorus in the Greek theatre always and invariably wore masks, and these indicated gender, age, and social status. So to some extent did the costumes, which were generally rather ornate. The *skeuopoios* will have also met special requirements such as the coverings of the suffering Heracles in *Deianeira* and the rags and bandages of Philoctetes. There were some conventional portable props, for example kings carried a staff of authority, military men had swords, and so forth. But otherwise stage-props were employed only sparingly, and this would make them all the more imbued with potential significance. Sophocles made something of a speciality of significant stage-objects that carried power as symbols or tokens within the dramatic fabric. Two examples from these three plays are the metal case in which Deianeira packs the robe that she sends to Heracles in *Deianeira*, and the bronze urn which is supposed to contain the ashes of Orestes in *Electra*.

The Sounds of Greek Tragedy

In such a large theatre the actors (three for each playwright) must have been skilled at making large, clear, and role-appropriate movements; and the chorus were highly rehearsed for their dancing. But there was also a great emphasis on the quality of sound. Actors were especially famed for their voices, which would have to vary from role to role; and the chorus were highly trained in singing as well as dancing. These performative skills were essential to the formal structure and aural textures of the whole genre. Throughout the fifth century there were within tragedies three main modes of vocal delivery: spoken iambics, sung choral lyric, and lyrics shared between chorus and actors.[18]

The plot, in the sense of the action and argumentation of the story, was predominantly carried by the three actors, though with usually only two directly contributing at any one time. Their parts were nearly all delivered in the spoken metre, the iambic trimeter, a line of usually twelve syllables. This was used both for dialogues and for speeches of widely varying length, sometimes running to forty lines or more. The chorus also contributes occasionally to these spoken scenes, but was always limited to a few lines; and for these spoken parts they were very probably represented collectively by the single voice of their leader. This is in keeping with the way that the reasoned, argumentative matter of the drama is the territory of the individual characters, not of the chorus. In Sophocles the spoken iambic sections tend to take up about three-quarters of the entire play, as reckoned by the (rather crude) measure of the number of lines.

Every play incorporated a chorus, a feature which was of the very essence of the art-form. This group of singer-dancers belonged within the created world of the play, and while it was common for them to be local inhabitants, their identity was a matter of choice for the playwright. The contribution of the chorus is developed through their role as involved witnesses; it is, in effect, to articulate a group response to the unfolding drama.[19] They are not tied down by the

[18] Further on this topic see the section 'On this Translation' on pp. xxvii–xxviii below.

[19] There has been endless discussion of the role of the chorus (not helped by a particularly vague couple of sentences in Aristotle's *Poetics*). So this paragraph is no more than an attempt at distillation.

specific individuality and rationality that are intrinsic to the roles of the speaking actors. In a nutshell, the chorus always attempts, by means of its poetic and musical resources, to face what has happened, or may be about to happen. They do their best to make some sense of the events unfolding before their eyes. They are never silenced or reduced to inarticulacy: on the contrary they order their responses and thoughts into poetry, song, and dance. This highly crafted re-visioning of the events of the play adds a whole extra dimension to the texture of the dramatic matter, a layering that cannot be reached through the speech or person of a single character.

The primary vocal contribution of the chorus as a group took the form of dance-poems sung in lyric metres, and accompanied by a double-pipe wind instrument, the *aulos.* These songs (or 'odes') are interspliced with the sections of the play spoken by the actors. They are mostly arranged in stanza-pairs of some ten to fifteen lines, although there are also some stand-alone stanzas. They were all set in complex metres, every stanza-pair unique.[20]

In addition to the spoken acts and the choral songs, there is a third distinct mode of expression, which may be covered by the loose term 'lyric dialogue'. There are one or two (occasionally more) of these lyric dialogues in every tragedy: they involve the chorus and one (rarely two) of the actors singing in lyric stanzas, but contributing in widely varying proportions. Crucially, they are not as a rule positioned in between the spoken acts, as the odes are, but are an integrated part of the action of the play. So they do not stand apart like the purely choral songs, but are caught up in the main current of events. While they occur in a variety of circumstances, they all come at junctures of heightened emotional intensity, often but not invariably of distress. It is as though they break through the constraints of the measured and rational iambic speech (and they do sometimes include some iambic lines within the lyric structure).

Finally, and less distinctively than these three modes, there are occasional passages of 'recitative' metres (anapaests and trochaics) which are pitched somewhere in between iambic and lyric. These

[20] A clutch of technical terms has accumulated around choral songs. The first entrance-song is conventionally called the 'parodos', and each of the others is known as a 'stasimon'. We do not really know, however, what these terms signify. The same goes for the labelling of stanza-pairs as 'strophe' and 'antistrophe', and the stand-alone stanzas as 'epodes'.

are usually delivered by the chorus-leader, and often accompany arrivals and departures. These intermediate types of delivery are also particularly used to signal a quickening pace as the final movement of the play approaches.

In conclusion, we encounter a huge theatrical space, where both the sight and the sound of the tragedies played were presented in all their measure and beauty. Fine costumes and handsome masks, skilled dancing, mellifluous voices, gripping rhetoric, highly crafted poetry, both spoken and lyric, combine in a *Gesamtkunstwerk* (an 'all-in work of art'). Yet at the same time, the events and issues of the plays, with their deceptions, feuds, disappointments, cruelties, untimely deaths—all these are far from beautiful and far from comforting. Pain, anguish, conflict, mortality, the turbid ebb and flow. . . . Antigone's obsession with the dead, Creon's crushing inflexibility, Deianeira's jealous desperation, the injustice of the gods witnessed by Hyllus, Electra's obsessive vindictiveness, the threatening of insoluble dynastic contamination. . . . Such are the pains and distortions and instabilities of Sophoclean tragedy. And yet they do not deteriorate into cacophony or disgust or incoherence or silence: they face the music, and through that the suffering is itself turned into the coherence of song and poetry.

ON THIS TRANSLATION

THIS translation is, like the plays of Sophocles, in verse. It tries to do justice to both the sound of the poetry and the theatricality of the tragedies; it aims to flow through reading towards realization in action and sound. The rhythmical language aspires, in other words, to be spoken and enacted; and the wording seeks to infuse musicality and physicality into the dramatic texture as a whole.

There is a widespread supposition, especially in Britain, that plain prose keeps somehow 'closer' to the original Greek, and that unobtrusive modesty is somehow more 'faithful'. It is my view, on the contrary, that by turning what is variegated into monochrome, and what is polyphonic into monotone, such translations become essentially alienated from their originals. Joseph Brodsky wrote:[1] 'Translation is a search for an equivalent, not for a substitute. . . . A translator should begin his work with a search for at least a metrical equivalent of the original form.' I strongly agree, and this means abandoning the safe pedestrian homogeneity that is the hallmark of so many modern translations. Poetry calls for poetry, or, at the very least, for crafted verse.

There are, in fact, two quite different kinds of verse within Greek tragedy, as was initially explained on p. xxiv above. In keeping with Brodsky's tenet, I have striven for two quite distinct measures in English. About three-quarters of each Sophocles play is set in the spoken metre of Greek drama, the iambic trimeter, a line of twelve syllables on an iambic base.[2] At first sight this may look remarkably similar to the ten-syllable line of English blank verse, but, in fact, the 'short/long' patterning of ancient Greek is a very different dynamic from the 'weak/strong' patterning of English. Ancient Greek verse was not stress-based, as is English (and modern Greek), but was based on syllable-lengths. It is not easy for us (Anglophones) to sense how such patterning could provide form and musicality, but it is indisputable that that is how it was. Despite this fundamental difference, I have

[1] In a 1974 review of versions of Mandelstam.

[2] This consisted of three blocks of four syllables in the grouping of 'long or short/long/short/long'. The long syllables could be broken into two shorts in places to make a total of thirteen or fourteen syllables in the line.

still found that, for me, the English stressed iambic is the best metrical equivalent for the Greek quantitative iambic.[3] I have set up a pulse that is basically iambic, but with no regular line length, and anything between four and fourteen syllables in a line. Quite frequently ending a line between a weak and a strong syllable also serves to break up any metronomic regularity of the beat.

The remaining portions of the tragedies, a quarter or so, are nearly all set in highly complex and patterned measures, conveniently labelled as 'lyric' (see also above, pp. xxv–xxvi). Most of these, the 'odes', were composed to be performed by the chorus in unified song, but there are also some lyrics which are shared in a kind of 'lyric dialogue' between actors and chorus. So far as metre and poetry are concerned, however, they are generally like the songs, not like the spoken iambics. Most, though not all, of both these kinds of lyric are arranged in pairs of metrically identical stanzas, presumably sung and danced identically, even though they can be quite contrasting in tone and subject-matter.[4] Tellingly, no two stanza-patterns in the whole of surviving tragedy are completely the same; we have, that is to say, several hundred pairs of stanzas, and every single pair is metrically unique.

Complex verses like this, made for setting to music, are not standard in English poetry, so any metrical equivalent is bound to be technically very different.[5] Most song-lyrics in English—from Elizabethan airs to hymns to modern musicals—are organized in fairly short stanzas with clearly marked rhythms. This verse-form is generally what I have gone for in order to achieve something of the equivalence that Brodsky called for. I do not pretend that my verse-forms and rhythms have any direct technical link with Sophocles' original metrics. I have arrived at them in a rather intuitive way, usually by letting some English phrases mull around in my mind until they coalesce into a ground-pattern on which to build.

[3] I have generally avoided clusters of actual blank verse, because it brings such burdens of association both with Shakespeare and other great poets of the past. I have probably fallen into all too many echoes in any case.

[4] These are conventionally known as 'strophe' and 'antistrophe', but since these terms mean little to us, I prefer to speak simply of 'pairs of stanzas'.

[5] The matching of the long syllables of lyric to stressed syllables in English is even less equivalent than with spoken iambics. It has been attempted, and has pedagogical value, but it produces patterns of syllables that do not carry any recognizable musicality in English.

These verse-forms are much simpler than the Greek measures, but they can at least aspire to musicality, audibility, and accessibility. More often than not I have also exploited rhymes, or half-rhymes, or off-rhymes of one kind or another. I have been encouraged in this by something of a renaissance of rhyming and tight verse-forms in the poetry in English of our times.[6] And rhyme has, after all, been perennially used in popular song of all periods. And tragic lyrics were the popular song of their day.

But what other features of Sophocles' verbal and dramatic craft call for some kind of equivalent in translation? Above all, what about 'diction'? What kind of level and tone and crafting of language is called for to give some idea of the expressiveness of the Greek? Again there is the basic division between the spoken iambics and the sung lyrics. Aristotle in his *Poetics* observes that the iambic metre is 'particularly speakable'. This is an important pointer; but, at the same time, it does not mean that the iambic parts are naturalistically imitative of everyday talk. The diction of tragic iambics is constantly expressing things in slightly unexpected, unordinary ways that heighten or sharpen its blend of meaning. While many of the lines are made out of everyday words, they are not put together in everyday ways. This is particularly true of Sophocles, and it is a difficult challenge to reflect this in translation.

There is also a scattering of higher-flown phrasing and vocabulary, and some word-forms that occur only in poetry. The Greek embraces both the colloquial and the poetical; it positively refuses a bland, unperturbed diction. I try to match this unpredictability in my translation. While I do not want to produce incongruities which stick out like a sore thumb, I do seek variety of tone and level; and I do not hesitate to use phrases and vocabulary that may surprise.[7] It is a standard negative criticism levelled at translations that they include turns of phrase that are either too low in diction, or too high, according to the taste of the reviewer. But this easy complaint is not necessarily valid, because such variability is there in the original.

[6] Including by some of the poets I most admire. I have been particularly influenced by Tony Harrison and Seamus Heaney in their versions of Greek tragedies—although I would not claim for a moment to be in their league.

[7] Robert Frost and Edward Thomas may lurk at the back of my consciousness, as I search for diction and phrasing that is in plain language and yet comes out with unpredictable and telling turns and colours.

No one would dispute that the spoken parts of any translation of Greek tragedy should be 'speakable'. That claim usually, however, means no more than that they are evenly worded and avoid phonetically awkward turns of phrase. I aspire to something more than that, which also makes the speech 'listenable' as well as speakable. Plain homogenous lines do not sustain attention: for Sophocles' spoken lines to come alive in English, some strangeness is needed, some twist, some grit. I hope that my verses will give people phrasings to be accentuated and relished out loud, something to 'get their mouth around'. I would even encourage readers to speak the words under their breath as they go along. Or, even better, gather in groups or classes or workshops and perform them out loud.

The sung lyrics are expressed in an appreciably more artful poetic register, and are even harder to capture in an English equivalent. They use a fair few rare and high-flown wordings, often put into quite twisted and artificial phrasings—indeed, they tend towards being 'difficult'. At the same time they still cohere as a challenging train-of-thought, and it would be a serious mistake to think of them as inaccessible to their audiences. A long and strong tradition of choral lyric in ancient Greece at religious and other ceremonial occasions meant that people were highly attuned to this kind of language and to its oblique thought-sequences. The lyrics were also undoubtedly audible. The organization of the Greek theatre budgeted for long rehearsal periods, and these prepared audibility and comprehensibility as high priorities. So I have attempted to find line-shapes and stanza-forms in English that allow the diction to be rich and strange, while at the same time restraining it from floating off towards the inflated or weird. My lyrics are considerably less challenging and less intricately crafted than the originals (and may sometimes be more doggerel than poetry!), but that is the price of making accessibility and audibility into priorities.[8]

The other consideration to be always borne in mind is the fact that the lyrics of tragedy were originally set to music, and were sung and danced. So musicality, or rather 'musicability', is something else to be worked into the translation-blend so far as possible. I have moulded

[8] Seamus Heaney sent this advice to an American director of his *Cure at Troy*: 'I'm devoted to the notion of each word being heard clearly by the audience. Bell-bing it into the ear, then carillon to your heart's content.'

them in the hope that these versions of the lyrics might one day be set to music and sung.

As well as these matters of metre and diction, there is the further crucial requirement of performance and performability. Although this version has been made for publication, it still conveys, I hope, the powerful theatricality of Sophocles. I have done my best to pitch the words so that they are not just compatible with being acted out on stage, but so that they might be positively integrated, and indeed mutually enhancing, with embodiment as well as with delivery. I have also followed the usual convention of adding stage-directions (see further p. xxxv below).

Greek tragedies were all-embracing artworks. They inextricably combined poetry, music, dance, movement, speech, spectacle. No translation can do justice to all of this ever-shifting multiformity, but there is, surely, some value in the attempt.

NOTE ON THE TEXT AND CONVENTIONS

THE manuscripts of Sophocles' plays were hand-copied for about a thousand years, and then neglected for much of the next nine hundred, before they were securely put in print at the end of the fifteenth century. It is not surprising that there is a scatter of miscopyings and errors in our few important medieval manuscripts. Nevertheless, the text seems to be largely intact, and it is mostly agreed upon among scholars; the places where a corrupt or disputed reading is serious enough to have a significant impact on a translation like this are fairly few and far between. I have generally followed the Oxford Classical Text (see Select Bibliography), but have felt free to disagree with it; and I have raised what I regard as the most important textual questions in the notes to the lines in question.

The kind of possible corruption of the text that makes the most impact on a translation is post-Sophoclean additions to the text, usually known as 'interpolations'—so far as they can be detected. Their extent is much disputed, and some scholars believe they are widespread—even as much as one line in every fifty on average—while others insist that there are very few, if any. I am one of those who believe that there are quite a lot, mostly very few lines in length, scattered through our texts. The great majority of these will have been added by actors in the fourth century, in order to elaborate their parts. This is not at all an implausible scenario because the plays went through a century and more of being widely performed professionally throughout the Greek world. And we know that the actors changed and adapted the texts because the Athenians eventually attempted to establish an 'authorized version'.

The problem is that detecting these interpolations inevitably involves a high degree of subjective judgement. The main justification is bound to be the detection of alleged problems or anomalies in the text as it is transmitted. But this method tends to imply that everything that is authentic Sophocles is perfect, and that everything that has been added is somehow intrusive or incompetent. This is obviously a highly dubious business, but there is, nonetheless, no avoiding the challenge. I have attempted to make up my own mind on such issues, and wherever I think there is a serious possibility of interpolation, I have raised that in the notes to the passage in question.[1] Where I believe that interpolation is highly probable (certainty is impossible), I have put square brackets (i.e. [. . .]) around the lines in question. I would encourage readers simply to jump over those lines.

Omissions of bits of Sophocles from the transmitted text (as opposed to additions) are far less widespread; editors have tended to be too ready to suppose that a line or lines have been lost merely in order to account for some minor problem or other. It remains true, however, that there are a few places where this is the most likely explanation of something that has evidently gone wrong with the text as handed down to us. In those places where I take this to be the best solution, I have added some words of my own to give the gist of the missing bit, and have put them between angled brackets (i.e. <. . .>). There are also occasionally places where some lines have very probably become displaced and need to be transposed back to where they originally belonged.

In addition to such textual issues, there are some recurrent problems which have to be faced by any translator, whatever the nature and style of the version. A particularly prominent one is the spelling of proper names. It might seem at first glance that the names should simply be transliterated from the Greek, since this would be closest to the original. But in practice this is over-alienating, because many of the names have become familiar in adapted spellings. This is most obvious with place-names, such as Thebes for *Thebai*, Troy for *Troia*, etc. English has also traditionally used Latin spellings for other proper names. In many cases it would be easily acceptable if these were returned to their Greek spellings, e.g. Elektra, Haimon, Olympos, etc. The trouble is that there are others which would seem obtrusively strange, and some that would strike most readers as outlandish—some blatant examples are Oidipous, Klytaimestra, and Mykenai, long familiar as Oedipus, Clytemnestra, and Mycene. So I have (with some reluctance) taken the easy way out and used the standard Latin spellings in nearly all cases.

There are some other relatively minor recurrent features which pose particular problems for translation. One is insults and abuse: it is very hard to find equivalents across languages, which carry the

[1] There are two particularly important such passages in these plays: *Antigone* 905–12 and *Electra* 1505–7. See notes to p. 203 and pp. 222–3.

same kind of tone and level of aggression without being too crude or too stilted. If only English still used 'villain'! Another is interjections, i.e. places where characters utter sounds that are non-verbal: cries of pain or grief, and also of surprise or joy. Modern English is largely lacking in conventional interjections of grief ('alas' and 'ai me' have become archaic); and the most common interjections in Greek—such as *oimoi*, *papai*, *aiai*, *iou*, *e e*—do not generally have phonetic matches in English. Some translators resort to the solution of simply transliterating, but to my ear the resulting sounds are over-intrusive. In many places I have simply attempted to use one of the interjection-like phrases still current in English today, such as 'ah', 'oh no!'; in others I have thought it better to replace the Greek interjection with a stage-direction, such as '(*cries of pain*)'.

Finally there is the whole issue of what textual aids the translator should add to help the modern reader. The most prominent is stage-directions. I have followed the usual convention of including them in italics. It would be positively unfriendly to the reader not to do so; also it would dampen the awareness that this is a text made for performance. At the same time it needs to be stated clearly that our Greek text has no explicit stage-directions as such; in other words, all those included in this version are my own editorial additions. These are not proposals for a modern performance: all I have tried to do is to work out the likely stagings of Sophocles' own first performance, and have envisaged them as set within the general space of the ancient Greek theatre, as briefly laid out on pp. xxi–xxii above.

I have applied the basic working assumption that when stage-action is important in a Greek tragedy it is clearly implied and signalled in the text. This thesis (which I argued for in *Greek Tragedy in Action* and elsewhere) is not, however, above challenge. And even assuming it is justified, modern productions do not—and should not—regard themselves as bound by it. This means that I have limited printed stage-directions to those which I feel are pretty securely justified.[2] It should not need saying that stage-directions can have a very significant bearing on interpretation, and I have discussed these, especially those that are open to serious dispute, in the notes.

I have broken with the usual editorial convention by adding scene-headings and numbers (e.g. 'Scene 4'), and similar indications

[2] I have not included every minor indication that is evident from the wording.

for choral songs and lyric dialogues (e.g. 'Second Choral Song'). Most modern editions and translations have no scene-headings at all; some, however, follow an arcane analysis and numbering which obscure more than they help.[3] The scene-divisions added here may, I hope, help readers and performers to have a clearer idea of the play's construction. I should emphasize, though, that they are the product of my own structural analysis, and have no higher authority.

Finally, the marginal line-numbers are another editorial addition. It should also be made clear that the numeration is that of the Greek text, as is uniform in modern editions. This is not by any means consistently matched by the number of the lines in this translation.

[3] The technical terms 'prologue', 'episode', 'stasimon', 'kommos', and 'epilogue' are derived from a pedantic section of Aristotle's *Poetics*, which is probably not even the work of Aristotle himself.

SELECT BIBLIOGRAPHY

This Bibliography is mainly restricted to accessible works in English, particularly those which have been found most helpful.

Greek Tragedy in General

P. Easterling (ed.), *The Cambridge Companion to Greek Tragedy* (Cambridge, 1997).
H. Foley, *Female Acts in Greek Tragedy* (Princeton, 2001).
J. Gregory (ed.), *A Companion to Greek Tragedy* (Maldon, MA, 2005).
E. Hall, *Greek Tragedy: Suffering under the Sun* (Oxford, 2010).
H. Roisman (ed.), *The Encyclopedia of Greek Tragedy* (London, 2013).
R. Rutherford, *Greek Tragic Style* (Cambridge, 2012).
R. Scodel, *An Introduction to Greek Tragedy* (Cambridge, 2010).
O. Taplin, *Greek Tragedy in Action* (London, 1978).

Sophocles

TEXTS

R. Dawe (Teubner, Leipzig, 1975; 3rd edn, 1996).
H. Lloyd-Jones and N. Wilson (Oxford Classical Texts, Oxford, 1990).
H. Lloyd-Jones (Loeb, Cambridge, MA, 1994).

BOOKS WHICH INCLUDE CHAPTERS ON INDIVIDUAL PLAYS

F. Budelmann, *The Language of Sophocles* (Cambridge, 2000).
B. Knox, *The Heroic Temper* (Berkeley, 1964).
A. Markantonatos (ed.), *Brill's Companion to Sophocles* (Leiden, 2011).
S. Nooter, *When Heroes Sing: Sophocles and the Shifting Soundscape of Tragedy* (Cambridge, 2012).
K. Ormand (ed.), *A Companion to Sophocles* (Maldon, MA, 2012).
K. Reinhardt, *Sophokles* (3rd edn, Frankfurt, 1947; English tr. Oxford, 1979).
D. Seale, *Vision and Stagecraft in Sophocles* (Chicago, 1982).
C. Segal, *Tragedy and Civilization: An Interpretation of Sophocles* (Cambridge, MA, 1981).
R. Winnington-Ingram, *Sophocles: An Interpretation* (Cambridge, 1980).

ANTIGONE

Commentaries

R. Jebb (Cambridge 1900; reissued Bristol, 2004).

A. Brown (Warminster, 1987).
M. Griffith (Cambridge, 1999).

Articles etc.

D. Cairns, *Sophocles: Antigone* (London, 2016).
H. Foley, 'Tragedy and Democratic Ideology: The Case of Sophocles' *Antigone*', in B. Goff (ed.), *History, Tragedy, Theory* (Austin, TX, 1995), 131–50.
S. Goldhill, 'Antigone and the Politics of Sisterhood', in S. Goldhill (ed.), *Sophocles and the Language of Tragedy* (Oxford, 2012), 231–48.
C. Sourvinou-Inwood, 'Assumptions and the Creation of Meaning', in *Journal of Hellenic Studies*, 109 (1989), 131–48.

Reception

G. Steiner, *Antigones* (Oxford, 1984).
E. Mee and H. Foley (eds), *Antigone on the Contemporary World Stage* (Oxford, 2011).
S. Wilmer and A. Žukausaitė (eds), *Interrogating Antigone in Postmodern Philosophy and Criticism* (Oxford, 2010).

DEIANEIRA (TRACHINIAN WOMEN)

Commentaries

R. Jebb (Cambridge, 1892; reissued Bristol, 2004).
P. Easterling (Cambridge, 1982).

Articles etc.

L. Bowman, 'Prophecy and Authority in the *Trachiniae*', in *American Journal of Philology*, 120 (1999), 335–50.
P. Holt, 'The End of the *Trachiniae* and the Fate of Herakles', in *Journal of Hellenic Studies*, 109 (1989), 69–80.
R. Kane, 'The Structure of Sophocles' *Trachiniae*', in *Phoenix*, 42 (1988), 198–211.
B. Levett, *Sophocles: Women of Trachis* (London, 2004).

ELECTRA

Commentaries

R. Jebb (Cambridge, 1894; reissued Bristol, 2004).
J. March (Warminster, 2001).
P. Finglass (Cambridge, 2007).

Articles etc.

J. Billings, 'Orestes' Urn in Word and Action', in M. Telò and M. Mueller (eds.), *The Materialities of Greek Tragedy* (London, 2018), 49–62.

R. Kitzinger, 'Why Mourning Becomes Electra', in *Classical Antiquity* 10 (1991), 298–327.

M. Lloyd, *Sophocles: Electra* (London, 2005).

L. MacLeod, *Dolos and Dikê in Sophocles' Electra* (Leiden 2001).

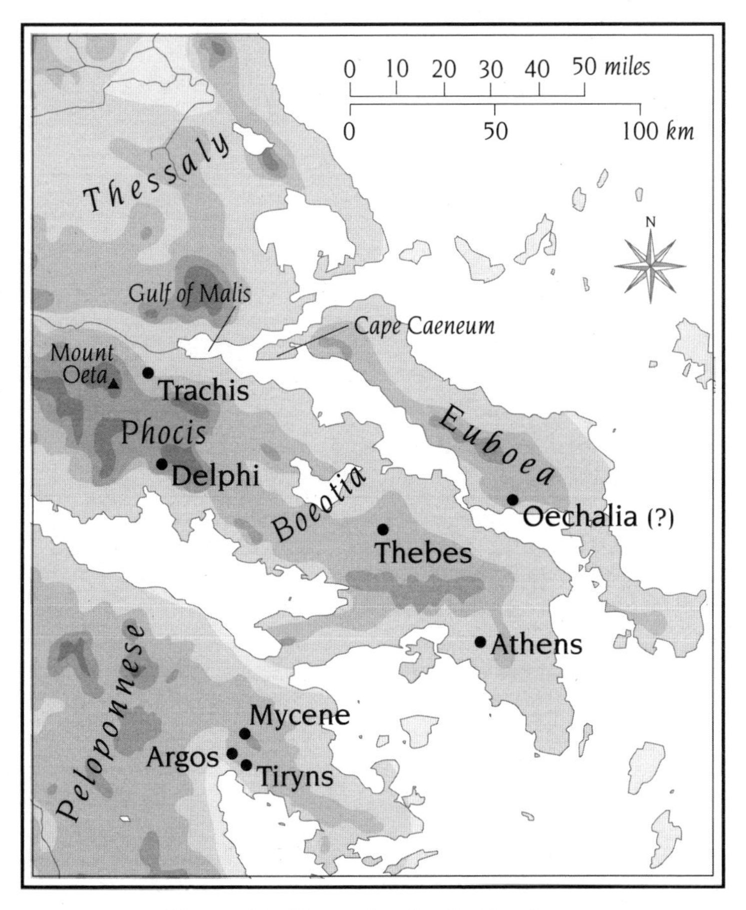

Places of significance for plays in this volume

ANTIGONE

INTRODUCTION TO *ANTIGONE*

The Invention of Antigone Herself

Antigone is an icon of Greek Tragedy; and Antigone is herself an icon of World Tragedy. Yet it is pretty sure that she was the creation of Sophocles. Long before him there were many stories about the royal house and the dynastic wars at Thebes that were told in epic poetry and other narrative forms. These included accounts of how Polynices, the exiled son of Oedipus, went to Argos and raised 'the Seven', an army with seven contingents and seven leaders to take over Thebes. They told how he and his brother Eteocles were implacable rivals, and how they killed each other in the battle where the defending Thebans were victorious. There were also stories about how the dead bodies of the invaders were left unburied until foreign intervention rescued them.[1] But, so far as we can tell, it was entirely Sophocles' innovation to have a sister who faced death in order to ensure the burial of Polynices. As part of this narrative plot he also invented her betrothal to Creon's son Haemon, and the suicide of his mother Eurydice.

Once invented, Antigone seems to have become almost immediately a favourite figure in the tragic stories of Thebes. Within Sophocles' own lifetime she has substantial roles in Euripides' *Phoenician Women*[2] and in Sophocles' own *Oedipus at Colonus*, composed probably some thirty-five years after *Antigone*. And a whole final scene of some seventy-five lines was added on to the end of Aeschylus' *Seven against Thebes*, bringing her on with a role and portrayal closely modelled on the prologue of Sophocles' play.[3] And we know that *Antigone* went on to be one of the best known and most reperformed of his plays. It is prophetically apt that in the play Haemon reports to his father that the people of Thebes are asking in support of Antigone 'does she not

[1] The Athenians claimed credit for this according to Euripides' tragedy *Suppliants* and other earlier plays now lost.

[2] Euripides also composed his own *Antigone* (now lost), which made deliberate departures from the Sophocles, while taking over his new heroine. We know little for sure except that by the time of the action Antigone and Haemon were married and had a son.

[3] We do not know when this was added but very likely (I believe) within fifty years of Sophocles' play.

deserve a crown of golden honour?' (line 699). While she is not given any communal recognition within the play—no monument or cult, for example—there is a sense in which the whole history of Tragedy has awarded her this crown.

Antigone has, indeed, serious claims to be the best-known and most discussed of all Greek tragedies. George Steiner[4] suggested that it was the prime tragedy for the nineteenth century, but was supplanted by *Oedipus the King* in the twentieth. But for the last thirty years—and arguably for the last seventy—*Antigone* has probably been more widely engaged with and performed, and in a wider range of places globally,[5] than any other play from before Shakespeare.

It is impossible to do justice to the multitude of those who have led engagements with *Antigone* in modern times, but a hasty roll-call of names will give some idea. Thinkers from Hegel to Jacques Lacan to Judith Butler (on gender); translators from Hölderlin to Seamus Heaney to Anne Carson; composers from Mendelssohn to Honneger to Theodorakis; playwright-adapters from Anouilh to Athol Fugard (*The Island* of 1973 is Robben Island under apartheid) to Femi Osofisan (1994); directors from Brecht to Andre Wajda (in 'Solidarity' Poland in the 1980s) to Ivo van Hove. Recent (2019) novels by Natalie Haynes and Kamila Shamsie and a film by Tacita Dean show that there is still more to come.

What is it then that gives the play such wide appeal? Big question! One reason may be that it dramatizes and gives a human embodiment to a whole range of fundamental issues, conflicts, and polarities. Steiner even claims a unique status in this regard: 'It has, I believe, been given to only one literary text to express all the principal constants of conflicts in the condition of man. These constants are five-fold: the confrontation of men and of women; of age and of youth; of society and of the individual; of the living and the dead, of men and of god(s).'[6] In keeping with this, I would suggest that it is this complex of interwoven confrontations that have made it possible for *Antigone* to be discussed and interpreted on so many different levels and in so many different cultures.

[4] His *Antigones* (see Bibliography) was a pioneer study in reception, surveying the many responses to Antigone from about 1790 to the 1980s.

[5] The book edited by Mee and Foley (see Bibliography) gives some idea of the extraordinary geographical extent of *Antigone*s in recent times.

[6] *Antigones*, p. 231.

The Double-Tragedy Construction

At the plainest level the play can be treated—and has been treated—as an idealistic parable of love versus hate, right versus wrong: the brave, clear-sighted young woman stands up as a martyr against inhumane oppression by authoritarian men. But it can also be viewed as much more complex and multi-layered. Not so much a clash of right and wrong, or even right and right,[7] so much as a shifting interplay of desires for life and for death, realms of above and below, love and rejection, individuality and social loyalty. . . . Not black and white, but not grey either.

And while the clash between Antigone and Creon is obviously at the core of the play, there are others who are powerfully and engagingly caught up in their struggle to the death; and these others offer different angles on the conflicts. They encompass Antigone's weaker sister Ismene; Haemon, torn between his father and his betrothed; Eurydice, mother more than wife; the guard caught between admiration for Antigone and saving his own skin; Tiresias the prophet who intervenes, but too late to change the movement towards death. And not least, the chorus of elders of the city, loyal to authority but nagged by doubts, trying—and far from succeeding—in making sense of the fatal events.

The more one looks closely at the whole play, the more un-simple it appears. It emerges as something more like a double-helix, and marked with many shifting colours rather than black and white. Among approaches to pulling together these complexities two may be particularly effective: through dramatic structure, and through the motivations of Creon and Antigone.

Consider first the play's construction. Antigone leaves the stage for the last time, after lamentations that clearly prefigure her death, at just over two-thirds of the way through (line 943). There is then a choral ode that reflects obliquely on her fate, and after that she is never again the focus of attention. The Tiresias scene is devoted entirely to his warnings to Creon; he never says anything direct about the rightness (or wrongness) of Antigone's case. Then in the Messenger's report, with Antigone already dead, the focus of the narrative is on

[7] A view often attributed to the great philosopher G. W. F. Hegel, although his actual views are more complex. Hegel is well discussed by Cairns (see Bibliography) 124–7.

Creon and through his viewpoint on Haemon. When Creon eventually returns (at line 1257 ff.) he has the body of Haemon with him: the body of Antigone is not alluded to, and presumably it was not seen, not in the original production at least. It would have been perfectly possible for Sophocles to have brought attention to the dead Antigone in the final part of the play, but he did not. Nor is there any suggestion of any kind of reminder, let alone memorial, for her.

The last quarter of the play is devoted to Creon. If the play were an unqualified heroization of Antigone, this would all be wasted time and trouble, with the audience impatiently feeling that 'it serves the bastard right'. The whole construction of the play clearly indicates, in other words, that it is 'about' Creon as well as Antigone, and concerned with Creon as an individual, not merely a token figure. Nelson Mandela saw this clearly when he organized a reading with his fellow-prisoners and took the part of Creon himself. Creon is, he appreciated, a study in the responsibilities of power and in the potential for disastrous mistakes.

It has even been suggested occasionally that Creon is the central character of the tragedy. This interpretation maintains that he is a man doing his level best to rule responsibly in difficult times, and that Antigone's role is secondary to this. She is, it is claimed, a menace, however courageous, against order, who brings the ruler down through her stubborn fanaticism. Advocates of this view emphasize the ancient Athenian attitude to women, especially the expectation that they should remain in the domestic space, and not let their voices be heard in public. So, they say, the audience of Athenian men will have unhesitatingly condemned Antigone, however admirable other ages may have found her.

But the whole structure of the play contradicts this interpretation as well. Antigone's case is given the first hearing through the opening prologue scene in such a way that it comes across as calling for some admiration, however dangerous. Then, whatever the pros and cons of her big confrontation with Creon (at lines 446 ff.), she clearly does not emerge from it discreditably. Next, the Haemon scene is crucial. The young man reluctantly exposes the weaknesses in his father's stance, and crucially reports (lines 692–700) what the citizens of Thebes are saying behind his back:[8]

[8] This tallies with Antigone's own claims at 504 ff.

For me, though, it's still possible to listen to
what's said in secret, and it's this:
the city's filled with sorrow for this girl
because, most undeservedly of women,
she is due to die most horribly—
and yet for highly admirable deeds.
She is the one who did not let her slaughtered brother
lie unburied, left for mutilation by wild dogs or crows—
so does she not deserve a crown of golden honour?
That's the sort of word that's darkly spread around.

Finally, and above all, there is her farewell scene, much of it in highly emotional lyric. This would be wasted on an audience that accepts Creon as in the right, regarding her as a mere rebel. This scene is recognizably 'tragic', clearly designed to bring the audience to tears. It may be open to dispute whether or not Creon is a tragic figure in his own way, but there can surely be no doubt that Antigone is.

Paired Flaws, Contrasting Flaws

Any straightforward taking of sides, any right-and-wrong approach, also breaks up even more under scrutiny of the motivations and dispositions of Creon and Antigone. The integrity of Creon's case, first, is the easier to unpick. Most of what he says in the first half of the play is unobjectionable, and even admirable.[9] Leaving the body of a traitor unburied, while open to question, was not incontrovertibly an illegal, let alone an impious, act. And it is not clearly wrong to insist that loyalty to the city, especially in times of war, trumps any loyalty to family. Yet, while there are not grossly offensive signs, there are naggingly alienating characteristics that begin to accumulate. He shows unjustified impatience, not least towards the conformist chorus. He is too hasty with accusations of financial bribery, and implausibly accuses the guard (as he will Tiresias later). He does not, as is often claimed, offend against conventional religion, and can plausibly claim to be reverencing the gods of the city. When, however, he says of Antigone (lines 486–9):

[9] His opening statement is cited with approval of its civic sentiments by the politician-orator Demosthenes about a hundred years later.

I do not care if she's my sister's child,
or closer kin than everyone who shares
our household Zeus, she and her sister
won't evade the nastiest of deaths . . .

he is failing to recognize that Zeus has a role as a guardian god of the family as well as of the city. And in the dialogue with Antigone, although he has all the physical power, he displays a growing obsession with the notion that she threatens to reverse gender-roles.

It is Ismene who first raises the consideration that Antigone is betrothed to Creon's son. His response is harshly crude (lines 568–9):

ISMENE
But are you going to kill your own son's bride?

CREON
I am—as there are other fields for him to sow.

After this it is the scene with Haemon in which the weaknesses in Creon's whole position are exposed. It becomes evident that, while he claims to represent the best interests of the city as a whole, it is really his own grip on power and his sense of his authority which drive him to his increasingly isolated stand. When he shows no respect at all for Haemon's courteous persuasion, the dialogue deteriorates, and deteriorates to Creon's disadvantage (lines 731–9):

HAEMON
I wouldn't tell you to exalt those who are in the wrong.

CREON
But isn't that the plague this woman is afflicted by?

HAEMON
The common people here in Thebes do not agree.

CREON
And is the city telling me the way to rule?

HAEMON
Can you not see how juvenile that sounds?

CREON
Is ruling here my task—or someone else's?

HAEMON
It's no true city that belongs to just one man.

CREON

And is the city not considered as its ruler's realm?

HAEMON

Well, you would make the perfect monarch of a desert land.

After this domineering over his son and his ruthless enforcement of Antigone's punishment, it is only to be expected that the prophet Tiresias will condemn Creon's judgement. And it is by now no surprise that Creon rejects the old seer with accusations of venal bribery. What is new is Tiresias' authoritative report that the gods above are being polluted by the unburied corpse. More fundamentally, he declares that the reason why Creon will be punished—and punished through his close family, not through the city—is that he has offended the gods below by breaking what appears to be a kind of cosmic order: the vertical division between the world in the sunlight above the ground and the world of Hades below (lines 1066–74):

> This is to pay for thrusting down below
> a human from this world above,
> resettling a living spirit in the tomb,
> whilst also keeping here above
> a corpse belonging to the gods below,
> unportioned and unburied and unhallowed.
> Yet these things are not for you to regulate,
> nor for the gods above: they have been
> violently displaced through your command.

So Tiresias finally confirms those grave faults that Creon will go on to recognize with such unreserved self-reproach in the final scene of the play. Up until the Tiresias scene the audience is likely to feel an increasing unease about his demeanour and behaviour, but not such outright condemnation. Creon has been deeply wrong, but also highly understandable. He is new to power in disturbed times, and it is far from incomprehensible that he makes the mistake of deciding that his authority must be maintained above all else. It is only human that the more his power is questioned, the more aggressively he asserts it. Some might question whether Sophocles has portrayed Creon with redeeming features enough to salvage tragic pity for him in the final scene, but that is evidently the way that the shape of the play flows.

Given, then, that Creon is deeply, if understandably, flawed, is Antigone unreservedly admirable? The more closely her motivation and self-justification are scrutinized, the more any pure model of virtue crumbles. 'Antigone-worshippers' maintain that she stands for love against hate and tyranny; her capacity for love is even claimed to extend to all humanity. But from the actual play, viewed without prejudice—especially prejudice coloured by Christianity—it emerges that Antigone does not express love for one single living being. She virulently rejects her sister Ismene; she never even hints at any personal feelings for Haemon.[10] There is a much-quoted sentiment that is claimed to express her benignity; but, once it is taken in context, it is clear that she is talking about her blood-kin, not about humanity at large. Line 523 does not mean 'I am born to join in love, not join in hate' but 'I'm bound by birth to join in love, not join in enmity'.

Antigone does indeed declare love, repeatedly and fulsomely: it is expressed for her dead family, above all her father, mother, and one brother, Polynices. In the prologue scene she even uses language that suggests an incestuous colouring (lines 72–6):

> It's right for me to do that and then die;
> belovèd I shall lie with him beloved,
> a righteous criminal.
> You see, I have to please the dead below
> for longer far than those up here
> as I shall lie down there for evermore.

Antigone's arguments and driving impulses are reserved for the dead and for the gods of the underworld below.

A significant element in promoting the general admiration of Antigone has been her piety, or at least her claims of piety. But her appeals to the gods turn out to refer mostly to the gods of the underworld, or the gods in general in relation to the dead. Even her celebrated speech on the 'unwritten statutes of the gods' (lines 450 ff.) is, when taken in dramatic context, more particular to her fixations, and less universal in scope. As Mark Griffith well puts it, 'her concern is not to distinguish and define the limits of secular authority, nor to articulate a coherent set of religious or political principles, but simply

[10] There would be a notable exception if Antigone were to speak line 572: 'Belovèd Haemon, how your father undervalues you!' But, apart from that being so out of keeping with the rest of her portrayal, the surrounding dialogue makes it clear that it was spoken by Ismene.

to defend her deeply-felt conviction that her brother and the gods below *must* be honoured, come what may—and she seems to be driven also by a virulent antipathy to Kreon himself'.[11]

There is another strand in Antigone's case which may appeal to some modern sensibilities, but in a way that derives from religions quite different from that of ancient Greece: the importance that Antigone attaches to her 'afterlife', her future existence with her family in death. This may well seem familiar and even admirable to those immersed in the traditions of Christianity or Islam. As well as the lines quoted above where she says she shall 'have to please the dead below | for longer far than those up here', she claims to know what the dead want and feel. For example she says to Creon (line 515), 'the man who's dead will not support that view'. And in her final speech she looks forward to being re-united below (897–901):

> At least as I reach there I am sustained by hoping
> I'll arrive as loving to my father,
> and beloved for you, my mother,
> and as loving towards you, dear brother.
> For all of you, when you lay dead, I washed
> and dressed and poured out
> funeral offerings with my own hands.

But in the Greece of Sophocles and of the great age of tragedy views of the 'afterlife' were very different from those of the Abrahamic religions. Hades was nothing like Paradise: the world below was usually envisaged as indistinct, dark, and comfortless. It was not even sure that the dead kept their characteristics or retained any memories from the world above. Sophocles' audiences would not have unquestioningly accepted Antigone's arguments about the paramount importance of affiliations among the dead, let alone their responses to the life that had been lived above by those arriving there. Arguably she is, like Creon, distorting the fundamental vertical order of the cosmos. Creon underrates the proper location of the living and the dead: Antigone overrates the lower reaches to the detriment of the living world above.

Antigone is not presented—not to my view at least—as a fully admirable, let alone lovable, person. There are stumbling-blocks in the way of sympathy for her. Or at least this is the case up until her final scene at lines 801 ff. It is her circumstances rather than her

[11] Commentary (see Bibliography) p. 200.

arguments that then capture the feelings of witnesses for her in the end. As she is brought under guard on the way to her subterranean cell, the old men of the chorus set the mood (lines 801–5):

> As I see this, even I am
> swept beyond the laws' high order.
> I can now restrain no longer
> teardrops spilling as I witness
> young Antigone here passing
> to the room where all must sleep.

In the course of the following lament-scene Antigone appeals repeatedly, not to any personal love for Haemon, but to that way she is being deprived of ever experiencing marriage. She shall only be wedded in death—she shall even be wedded to Death. She sums up her desolation at line 876: 'Without tears, without friends, without wedding-chorus . . .'. But at the same time she is granted the pity and the tears of spectators and readers, innumerable across the ages and the whole world. She has become an icon of Tragedy.

ANTIGONE

LIST OF CHARACTERS

ANTIGONE, daughter of Oedipus and Iocasta
ISMENE, Antigone's sister
CREON, the new supreme authority of Thebes, brother of Iocasta
GUARD, a Theban soldier
HAEMON, son of Creon, betrothed to Antigone
TIRESIAS, blind old seer of Thebes
MESSENGER, an attendant of Creon
EURYDICE, wife of Creon

CHORUS of elders of Thebes

Place: in front of the royal palace at Thebes. One side-direction leads to the civic areas of the city: the other goes towards the plain outside the walls, site of the battle fought the day before.

SCENE I (PROLOGUE)

°*Antigone and Ismene cautiously emerge together from the palace doors.*

ANTIGONE

My sister,° sister bound by blood, Ismene—
tell me this: of all the horrors left by Oedipus
what is there Zeus does not bring to a head
for us, the two still left alive?
All that's disastrous and distorted
and disgusting and humiliating—
all I've seen among our troubles, yours and mine.
And now what's this: this edict the Commander°
has just issued to the whole of Thebes?
Have you heard anything? Can you not know
that hostile dangers march on those we love? 10

ISMENE

°I've heard of nothing good or bad for them, Antigone,
not since the two of us were stripped
of our two brothers, slaughtered
on a single day by their two pairs of hands.
But since the Argive army's gone away last night,
I know of nothing after that to bring me either comfort,
or yet more disaster.

ANTIGONE

I thought as much: that's why I've fetched you here
beyond the outer doors, for you alone to hear.

ISMENE

What can it be?
It's clear you are fermenting some dark news. 20

ANTIGONE

Yes. Creon's granted one of our two brothers
burial with honour, while un-honouring the other.
Eteocles he's had interred with full observances
respected for the dead below:
but as for Polynices' wretched corpse,

a proclamation has been made to all the citizens
that nobody should lay him in the grave, or grieve for him;
but leave him all unwept, untombed,
rich pickings for the kites that relish carrion. 30
That's what they say our virtuous Creon
has ordained for you—and me, yes me!°
He's coming here to make this proclamation clear
to those who've not yet heard.
And he's not treating this as trivial, no:
death by public stoning° is prescribed
for anyone who does these things.
There: now it's up to you to show
if you are truly noble,
or, despite your blood, a coward.

ISMENE
If this is how things are, then what can I achieve
to tighten or to loosen them? 40

ANTIGONE
To share the effort, share the hazard? Think. . . .

ISMENE
What kind of danger? What can you be thinking of?

ANTIGONE
. . . to help these hands of mine to lift the corpse.

ISMENE
You mean to bury him?
Although it's publicly prohibited?

ANTIGONE
My brother—yes, your brother too,
want it or not. You won't find me betraying him.

ISMENE
Poor fool! When Creon has forbidden it?

ANTIGONE
It's not his place to separate me from what's mine.

ISMENE
O, sister, stop! 50

°Just think of how our father died, notorious, detested,
after he'd discovered his own crimes;
and how he jabbed his own two eyes himself.
And then his mother-wife, as she was both,
choked off her life hung in a twisted noose.
And third, our pair of brothers on a single day
fought on until they both were done to death
at one another's hands.
And now we two, the last two left—
look how our deaths would be the ugliest of all
if we defy the ruler's writ and power against the law. 60
We must remember we are born as women
and not made to fight with men;
and so we're subject to their stronger power.
That's why we have to bear these things—and even worse.
For my part, then, I'm going to beg forgiveness
from the dead, because I'm overruled by force,
and shall obey those in command.
There is no sense, I say, in trying
to do more than can be done.

ANTIGONE

Well then, I'll not press you—
and even if you ever wanted to take part,
I'd not be glad to have you acting with me. 70
You be the way that you see fit:
while I shall go and bury him.
It's right for me to do that and then die;
belovèd I shall lie with him beloved,°
a righteous criminal.
You see, I have to please the dead below
for longer far than those up here
as I shall lie down there for evermore.°
You, if you want, demean the things
the gods consider valuable.

ISMENE

I don't demean them.
But I've no ability to go against the city's will.

ANTIGONE

You may give that as your excuse: 80
but I am going now to raise a tomb
for my beloved brother.

She moves to go.

ISMENE

O god, I am so terrified for you, poor thing!

ANTIGONE

Don't fear for me: just set your own course straight.

ISMENE

At least tell no one what you're doing;
keep it secret. And I'll do the same.

ANTIGONE

No, no, speak out!
I shall dislike you all the more for staying quiet,
and not proclaiming this to everyone.

ISMENE

Your blood is hot for such spine-chilling things.

ANTIGONE

At least I know I'm pleasing those I most should please.

ISMENE

Yes, if you could succeed;
but you're in love with what's not possible. 90

ANTIGONE

When I have no strength left, that's when I'll stop.

ISMENE

You should not start to chase what can't be done.

ANTIGONE

Say that and earn my hatred,
and be rightly hated by the dead as well.
Leave me alone with my own foolishness
to suffer this, if it's so terrible.

I'll suffer nothing that's too bad
to stop me dying well.

ISMENE

Well, go then if you think that's right.
Your mission may be madness, yet, for sure,
you're truly loving towards those you love.

°*Ismene goes back inside; Antigone goes in the direction of the plain outside the city-walls.*
The chorus enters from the side of the city.

FIRST CHORAL SONG (PARODOS)

CHORUS

°Brightest ray that ever shone 100
on seven-gated Thebes,
golden eye of daylight, sunrise over Dirce's streams.
You reversed the Argive might
of bristling battle-gear,°
sent them off in panic flight
gored by our sharper spur.
They were launched against our land by 110
Polynices, roused through doubtful
quarrels°—like an eagle taking
wing across our country, shrieking,
with his threats against our city,
thick with spears and nodding crests.

So above our homes it stood
and gaped its spear-filled beak,
but, before gorged with our blood, 120
it turned tail and flew back.
And before flames licked our walls,
the battle-clatter shook,
and around its back there coiled
the hissing Theban snake.°

Zeus detests high-boasting bluster:
and so, when he saw them coming
with a stream of golden clatter, 130
he let fly his fire-bolt, hurling
down the one who scaled the ramparts
stifling his victory-cry.

He teetered and then plunged
thudding to the ground,
the man who brandished fire,
fanned with hate-filled wind
in his crazed attack.
But he falls and fails.°
And mighty Ares° crushed
yet others other ways. 140
Seven leaders, seven portals,
took their stand to face each other,°
left their bronze for Zeus of trophies.°
All except those cursèd brothers—
single father, single mother—
who both fixed their winner's spear-point
in the other, sharing death.

But Victory now has come,
glory matched by joys
for chariot-famous Thebes.°
Let's forget those wars, 150
erased by peace of mind;
visit every shrine
with night-long song and dance;
and, Bacchus,° lead the line.

°*Creon, with his bodyguards, comes out of the palace.*

Here, though, Creon is approaching,
our new leader in these latest
turns of fortune. What's he planning,
that has led him to convene this
special meeting of us elders? 160

SCENE 2

CREON

The city, gentlemen, has now been steadied
on an even keel, saved by the gods
from shipwreck in the violent storm.
And I have summoned you especially,
because I know you always paid
due homage to the rule of Laius;
and then to Oedipus when he was king;
then after he had died, you stood firm
by his sons with sound advice.
So now that they have fallen on a single day, 170
polluted, striking and struck down at their own hands,
it falls to me to take up sovereign power
through my close kinship° with the dead.
There is no way, say I, to know a man,
his spirit, mind, and judgement—all the man—
until he's shown his worth
in handling law and governance.
For in my view the one who runs the country,
yet does not hold firmly to best policy,
or keeps his mouth shut from some fear, 180
I've always held a man like that beneath contempt.
And I've no room for one who values
his own kin above his fatherland.
All-seeing Zeus now be my witness,
I would never hold my tongue
if I could see disaster looming for my fellow-citizens
to threaten their security; nor would I ever count
my country's enemy as kin to me.°
I recognize it's this that keeps us safe;
and it is only when we sail upon an even keel
that we can work out who our dear ones are. 190
It is through principles like these
I aim to make this city strong.
Accordingly I have proclaimed this edict
to the citizens concerning the two sons of Oedipus.

(delivering edict)
Eteocles, who perished fighting with distinction
for our country, shall be buried in the tomb
with all the rituals that should accompany
the noblest dead below.
As for his sibling, namely Polynices,
who returned from exile in the hope
of burning down his native land and family gods, 200
desiring to taste kindred blood,
and drag the rest away to slavery:
it has been publicly decreed that nobody
shall give him funeral rites, nor mourn for him.
His corpse must lie unburied
for the birds and dogs to rend,
a spectacle of shame.
Such is my way of thinking:
on my watch wrong-doers
never shall be rated higher than the just.
The man who stays true to this city shall,
in death and life alike, have honour due from me. 210

CHORUS-LEADER
You may do as you please, son of Menoeceus,
with those malignant to this land, and those benign.
You have the power to lay down any law you wish
in dealing with the dead and us who live.

CREON
Then see to it that my commands . . .

CHORUS-LEADER
Assign that task to someone younger . . .

CREON
No no, there are already guards to watch the corpse.

CHORUS-LEADER
What further order are you giving then?

CREON
Don't ever side with those who disobey.

CHORUS-LEADER

Who but a fool would long for death? 220

CREON

True, that's the penalty. Yet hope of payment
has so often dragged men down.

SCENE 3

Enter the guard suddenly but apprehensively from the side of the plain.

GUARD

°My lord, that I have come here swiftly,
out of breath or fleet of foot,
would not be true.
In fact I often hesitated on the way
and started to turn back.
My spirit held a lengthy dialogue:
'You fool, why tread the path to where
you'll meet with punishment?'
Then, 'Idiot, why have you stopped again?
If Creon finds this out from someone else,
you're certain to pay dear for it.' 230
The twists of suchlike thoughts held back my progress,
and a little way became a long, long trek.
But in the end arriving here has won the day—
for you. And I shall tell you why, no matter what:
I clutch onto the hope
that I can only suffer what is fated.

CREON

What's driving you to such a state?

GUARD

First I would like to tell you where I stand:
I did not do the deed; and did not see who did;
so it would not be right for me to come to any harm. 240

CREON

You're shrewd at setting fences round the matter:
clearly you have news.

GUARD

It's frightening to have to tell of fearsome things.

CREON

Well why not spit it out and then be on your way?

GUARD

All right, I'm telling you.
Someone's just buried it, the body;
sprinkled some dry dust on it,
and carried out the rituals, then gone.

CREON

What's this? What man° has dared to do this thing?

GUARD

I've no idea.
There was no trace of digging with an implement;
the ground was hard and undisturbed, 250
unmarked by any track of wheels—
whoever did it left no trace.
So when the first watch of the day found out,
it was a horrible surprise for everyone.
°The corpse had disappeared from sight,
not laid down in a grave, but covered with a layer of dust,
as though performed by someone to avoid pollution.
And there was no sign that any dog or predator
had come and mauled it.
Well, there were violent words between us then,
with guard accusing guard— 260
it might have come to blows,
with no one there to stop the brawl,
for everyone supposedly had done the act,
yet no one obviously had, or knew of anything.
We all were quite prepared to handle red-hot iron,
to walk through fire, swear by the gods
that we'd not done a thing, and had no knowledge
who had planned or carried out the deed.

But in the end, when we weren't getting anywhere,
someone proposed a thing that made us all
stare down in fear—we couldn't contradict the man, 270
yet couldn't see how it would do us any good.
He said it ought to be reported straight to you,
and not concealed. That won the day:
the shortest straw selected me to be the wretch
for this delightful task. So here I am—
though wanting this no more than I am wanted,
since nobody loves the bringer of bad news.

CHORUS-LEADER

My lord, I wonder if this act might not have been
directed by a god? That thought has kept on nagging me.

CREON

Stop there! Before you cram me full of rage, 280
and get shown up a fool as well as old.
Your notion is intolerable:
the gods might care about this corpse?
D'you think they covered him in recognition
of his benefactions?—the man who came
to set their temples and their offerings alight;
who came to rip apart their country and its rituals?
Or do you see the gods rewarding vicious men?
The answer's 'no'.
But there are people in this land who've long
been discontented, stirring talk against me secretly. 290
They toss their heads and will not keep their necks
beneath the yoke of being satisfied with me.
And I am certain that these guards have been
induced by bribes from them to engineer this burial.
°There is no currency between us humans
that is so corrupt as silver.
It is money ransacks cities, roots out people from their homes,
corrupts good minds to turn to vicious ways;
it's money's opened up to people every sort of wrong
and wickedness without restraint. 300
But those who've taken cash to do this thing
have made damn sure they'll pay the price eventually.

(*to the guard*) As I still keep my reverence for Zeus,
be sure of this—I speak on oath:
if you guards fail to find the perpetrators of this burial,
and bring them here before my eyes,
one death won't be enough for you:
you'll be strung up alive to demonstrate
just what this insolence° is bound to mean.
And so you'll know in future where
to take your handouts from, and realize 310
you should not look for pickings from just anywhere.
For shady dealings bring more people
crashing down than they leave staying safe.

GUARD

Permission now to speak? Or simply turn and go?

CREON

Can you not tell how much your words annoy me?

GUARD

And is the irritation in your ears or in your mind?

CREON

Why try to pinpoint where I feel the pain?

GUARD

The man who did it irks your mind: me just your ears.

CREON

You clearly are a great one for the clever talk. 320

GUARD

Maybe—but not the one who did this deed.

CREON

You did, and did because you sold yourself for silver.

GUARD

It's dreadful when decisions rest on false beliefs.

CREON

You're welcome to go on and on about beliefs,
but if you don't produce for me the men responsible,
you'll be a demonstration of the way
corrupted gain ends up with pain.

Creon goes off into the palace.

GUARD

Yes, let's hope he's found . . .
though whether found or not is up to chance:
what's certain, though, is that you'll not
be seeing me again.
It's more than I could hope
that I've got safe away this time— 330
for that I owe the gods much thanks.

The guard departs back towards the plain.

SECOND CHORAL SONG

CHORUS

°There are many formidable things,
but none more formidable° than
are human beings.
They sail over ocean's grey wastes
with southerly storm-winds between
towering waves.
And the god most primeval of all—
undying, unwearying Earth—
by turning the soil
they repeatedly rake her and tear,
as horses pull ploughs back and forth, 340
year after year.

The birds in thought-fluttering flocks
are captured in snares, and wild beasts
trapped by their tricks,
and the shoals of the fish in the sea
get entangled in spiralling nets—
man's ingenuity!
They've invented devices and wiles
to domesticate animals that
roam in the wilds; 350
the resolute mountain-bred ox
and shaggy-maned horse are controlled,
necks under yokes.

Humans have learnt the skills to use
language and reason quick as the breeze;
and attitudes that bind the town;
and shields from frost and pelting of rain.
This all-resourceful human creature,
short of resource for nothing in future! 360
Only from death there's no release—
though cures have been found from dire disease.

They turn their clever aptitude
sometimes to bad, and sometimes to good.
Those who honour the country's law,
revering the gods, raise their city secure:
yet there's no city° for someone veering 370
off into ways of error through daring.
May one committing things like those
not join in my thoughts, nor visit my house.

SCENE 4

The guard returns bringing Antigone as a prisoner.

CHORUS-LEADER
I'm bewildered by this portent:
there is no denying this is
young Antigone. O wretched
child of wretched father, what has 380
happened? Surely they're not bringing
you for disregarding royal
edicts, caught in something foolish?

GUARD
This is the one who did the deed,
arrested in the act of burying.
But where's Creon?

CHORUS-LEADER
Here, coming from the palace just as he is wanted.

CREON (*entering*)
What's going on? What's this that chimes with my arrival?

GUARD
My lord, there's nothing we should swear will never happen:
second thoughts can turn our first thoughts into liars.
So I was clear I'd never be back here, 390
not after all those threats you lashed me with.
But since there is no pleasure that can match
obtaining what you prayed for but could never hope,
I've come, although I swore I never would.
I'm bringing this young woman here:
we caught her in the act of burial rites.
No drawing straws this time:
this stroke of luck is mine and no one else's!
And now, my lord, it is for you to take her,
question, and convict her.
I'm a free man, and it's only right for me
to be discharged from this bad business. 400

CREON
How was it that you caught her? Where?

GUARD
She was there, burying the man. That's all there is to know.

CREON
D'you realize what you're saying? Are you sure?

GUARD
I saw her burying the corpse you had forbidden.
Is that loud and clear enough?

CREON
How was she found? How caught red-handed?

GUARD
Well, this is how it was.
Once we were back, fresh from those threats of yours,
we cleared the dry earth off the corpse,
and swept the rotting body well and truly bare. 410
We settled on the higher ground, up-wind
so that the stink of him did not get blown our way.
And we were wide awake, and cursing at each other,

making sure that no one got distracted from the job.
The time went by like this until the bright disc of the sun
had reached its zenith in the sky—and it was scorching hot.
°Then suddenly a whirlwind lifted up
a sky-high cloud of dust which swept the plain,
and ripped the foliage from the thickets there.
The whole wide air was filled with whirling grit: 420
we simply had to close our eyes,
and put up with this eerie torment.
It cleared up at long last—and there she was,
the girl, for all to see.
She was lamenting shrilly, like the screeching
of a bird that finds its nest is empty, chicks all gone:
that's how she cried out when she saw the body bare;
and kept on calling violent curses down
upon the heads of those who'd done this thing.
Then straight away she fetched dry dust
in her bare hands, and poured around the body 430
three libations from an urn of finely crafted bronze.
On seeing this we rushed and cornered her—
though she was not at all alarmed.
When we accused her of the earlier act
as well as this one, she did not deny a thing.
That caused me pain and pleasure both together:
it's very nice to have got free from trouble,
yet to drag down somebody who's dear instead—
that's painful.
But all this matters less to me
than does my own survival. 440

CREON (*to Antigone*)
You, yes you there, staring at the ground,
do you admit you did this, or do you deny it?

ANTIGONE
Yes, I admit I did, and don't deny the deed.

CREON (*to guard*)
You go, wherever you may please;
you're free, acquitted of this serious charge.

Exit guard.

SCENE 5

CREON (*to Antigone*)
And you, now answer me, and keep it short:
were you aware that doing this
had been forbidden by the proclamation?

ANTIGONE
I was aware. How could I not be? It was clear enough.

CREON
And still you dared to contravene these laws?

ANTIGONE
°I did, because for me it was not Zeus 450
who made this proclamation;
nor did Justice that inhabits with the gods below
decree these laws for humans to observe.
I have concluded that your edicts, as you're mortal,
are not strong enough to override
the statutes of the gods,
which are unwritten and unshakeable.
These do not date, you see, just from today
or yesterday, but live for ever,
and nobody knows when they first came to light.
So I was not prepared to pay the penalty
before the gods for breaking those,
not out of fear for any mere man's way of thinking.
I knew I had to die for it—of course I did— 460
that did not need your proclamation.
And if I die before my time, I count that as pure gain.
For one who lives amidst as much distress as me
can't help but see death as a gain.
And so, for me, this doom of yours is far from pain:
but had I left the body of my mother's son
unburied there, that would
have really hurt, while this does not.
And if you think I am a fool for what I've done,
the one who passes judgement on me is the fool. 470

CHORUS-LEADER

It's clear the daughter has derived
this fierce trait from her father's fierceness.
She has got no notion how to compromise in trouble.

CREON

Well, let me tell you: attitudes that are too rigid
are most likely to come crashing down,
and iron that has been forged to extra hardness
you will see most cracked and splintered.
I have known the most unruly horses broken
with a little bridle—and rightly so because
big thoughts are not allowed
in one who is a household slave.
She showed her expertise with insolence 480
back then when she defied official laws;
and after that here is a double insolence:
she laughs and revels over what she's done.
Now I'm no man, and she's the man,°
if this control of hers is going to stay unpunished.
I do not care if she's my sister's child,
or closer kin than everyone who shares
our household Zeus,° she, and her sister too,
will not evade the nastiest of deaths.
I sentence her as well, as being equally
involved in scheming for this burial. 490
Go summon her out here—I saw her
in the house just now, distracted and hysterical.
The mind that's plotting wrong in secret
often gets detected in advance;
and yet I hate it too when someone, after being caught,
attempts to paint the crime as beautiful.

ANTIGONE

So is there anything you want beyond just killing me?

CREON

No, nothing—having that's my everything.

ANTIGONE

Why are you waiting then?
I have no liking for a single syllable you say, 500

and trust I never shall—just as I'm bound
to keep on being disagreeable for you.
And yet . . . what higher glory could I win
than by performing my blood-brother's burial?
And all these people here would give me their approval,
were their tongues not clamped by fear.
One of the great advantages of one-man rule
is liberty to do and say just what you please.°

CREON

But you alone of all the Thebans see things in this light.

ANTIGONE

These do as well, but gag their mouths in front of you.

CREON

And are you not ashamed to think so differently? 510

ANTIGONE

No shame in honouring those born of one womb.

CREON

Did his opponent to the death not share your blood as well?

ANTIGONE

He did—same mother and same father too.

CREON

So how can you bestow a favour that besmirches him?

ANTIGONE

The man who's dead will not support that view.°

CREON

Not even if you honour him as equal to that filth?

ANTIGONE

It was his brother, not some slave, who died.

CREON

Out to destroy this land: the other stood in its defence.

ANTIGONE

Yet Hades still desires these funeral rites.

CREON

The good should not get equal treatment with the bad. 520

ANTIGONE
Who is to say what's seen as rightful in the world below?

CREON
An enemy can never be a friend, not even after death.

ANTIGONE
I'm bound by birth to join in love, not join in enmity.°

CREON
Then go below and love those there, if love you must.
No woman's going to be in charge as long as I'm alive.

Ismene is brought out under guard.

CHORUS-LEADER
Here's Ismene coming out now
weeping for her dearest sister.
Brooding storms lour on her forehead,
stain her lovely cheeks with teardrops. 530

CREON (*to Ismene*)
It's you who's lurked inside my house;
it's you has drained me like some viper;
and I was unaware that I was feeding up
two deadly threats to overturn my throne.
Speak up and tell me this:
Do you admit to sharing in this burial?
Or will you swear to ignorance?

ISMENE
I did it, yes—if she agrees.
I share the guilt and take the blame.

ANTIGONE
No. Justice will not let you make this claim.
You were unwilling, and I did not make you part of it.

ISMENE
But in your hour of need I'm not ashamed 540
to join you on your voyage of suffering.

ANTIGONE
No. Hades and the dead can tell whose deed it was.
I do not like a loved one who shows love with only words.

ISMENE

But, sister, don't deprive me of the right
to die with you and join in reverencing the dead.

ANTIGONE

Don't try to share my death; and don't lay claim
to things you did not touch. My dying will suffice.

ISMENE

Why should I want to live if I'm bereft of you?

ANTIGONE

Ask Creon that—he is the one you care about.

ISMENE

Why stab at me, although it does no good? 550

ANTIGONE

It hurts me too, if with my mockery I mock at you.

ISMENE

Well then, what way can I still do you good?

ANTIGONE

By your surviving. I do not begrudge you your escape.

ISMENE

Am I to be excluded from your death?

ANTIGONE

You are, because you chose to live, and I to die.

ISMENE

I spoke my honest mind at least.

ANTIGONE

And you strike some as right: to others I seem right.

ISMENE

And so our errors are judged equally.

ANTIGONE

Farewell. And live.
My life has long been dead, so I may serve the dead. 560

CREON

I'd say that one of these two girls
has just been seen as mad:
the other has been from the start.

ISMENE

Yes, in the worst of times, my lord, good sense
abandons even those endowed with it.

CREON

That's true of you: you chose to go along with criminals.

ISMENE

What life's worth living by myself and not with her?

CREON

Don't speak of 'her'—as she no longer is.

ISMENE

But are you going to kill your own son's bride?°

CREON

I am—as there are other fields for him to sow.

ISMENE

But not so closely suited as with him and her. 570

CREON

I hate the prospect of a bad wife for my son.

ISMENE

Beloved Haemon, how your father undervalues you!°

CREON

You and your marriage-match just make me furious!

ISMENE

So will you really leave your son deprived of her?

CREON

It's Hades who is going to call this marriage off.

ISMENE

It seems decided: she must die.

CREON

Yes, by both you and me.
(*to his soldiers*) Waste no more time, but take her inside, men.
From now they must be women, not let loose.
Even the brave, you know, attempt to run 580
when they see Hades looming close.

Antigone and Ismene are escorted inside; Creon stays on.

THIRD CHORAL SONG

CHORUS

°Happy the life that's lived
all untainted by taste of bad.
Utter disaster pours
on the family and the house
shaken by gods from above.
Just the way the rolling wave
stirred by a north-wind storm
moves sweeping above the gloom,
churning up from the bed 590
of the ocean the black silt cloud.
Loud on the headland shore
the ranks of the breakers roar.

From long ago the pains
of this dynasty° pile upon pains
constantly from the dead,
so the family cannot get freed;
always some god bears down
so they never can break the chain.
Oedipus' house was bright
with the light of its latest root: 600
now that has been cut through
by the blade of the gods below—°
bloodied by foolish speech
and by thoughts beyond reason's reach.°

Zeus, your rule is so commanding
that no human overstepping
could have strength to countermand it.
No, not sleep the all-enwrapping
nor long months can undermine it.
Never aged with time, almighty,
you hold rule on high Olympus,
lofty hall of dazzling brightness. 610
This is law as laid down sure for
past time, present, and hereafter:

nothing vast as this encounters
human life without disaster.°

Ranging Hope may bring to many
people benefits through wishing:
but for many it deceives them
with mere feather-brained ambition.
Unaware before they know it
their foot's smouldering° in hot embers.
Someone coined this well-known saying,
words which wisdom still endorses: 620
bad things seem like good to someone
whose perception alters after
god directs them to disaster.
They're not long without disaster.

SCENE 6

Haemon is seen coming from the direction of the city.

CHORUS-LEADER

°Here comes Haemon, youngest of your
children. Is he here in anger
at the sentence on Antigone
[his bride-in-waiting]
his affianced, incensed at
being cheated of his marriage? 630

CREON

We'll soon find out, and better than by guesswork.
(*to Haemon*) My son, now that you've heard the sentence
firmly fixed against your bride-to-be,
have you come here enraged against your father?
Or do I stay still dear to you, whatever I may do?

HAEMON

Father, I remain your son,
and so, as long as you set out for me
sound judgements, I shall follow them.
For me no marriage shall be valued higher
than your guidance, when it's good.

CREON

That's right, my son: you should
wholeheartedly take up your stand in full support
behind your father's judgement. 640
This is why men pray to raise obedient offspring
in their homes: for paying back their enemies with harm,
and valuing their friends just as their father does.
All one can say about a man whose children
offer no support is that he's breeding problems
for himself—and hearty laughter for his enemies.
And so, my son, don't ever throw away your thinking mind
to gratify the pleasure that a woman gives;
you need to know that if you have a tainted wife
beside you in your bed at home,
then those embraces shall go cold. 650
What festering sore could there be worse
than having vicious kin?
So spit her out, this girl, this bitter poison—
let her mate with someone down in Hades.
I arrested her myself, you see, defying my commands,
the only one from all the city;
and I'll not present myself before the city
as untrue to my word: no, I shall kill her.
So let her go on with her chants of 'blood-kin Zeus'.°
If I raise my own family undisciplined,
then how much more will that be true of those beyond. 660
The one who's steadfast in his family affairs
will be perceived as just within the city too.
I'm confident that man would make an admirable ruler, (668)
and would be ready to be justly ruled;
and posted in the storm of battle 670
he would stay reliable, a trusty fellow-fighter.
°But the one who oversteps and violates the laws, (663)
or thinks that he can order those in charge around,
that person can no way earn praise from me.
Whatever man the city has established in authority,
he has to be obeyed in matters great and small,
in just and opposite alike.° (667)
There's nothing worse than breakdown of authority: 672

this is what ruins cities, shatters households,
scatters allied troops in flight:
obedience to authority keeps men secure in line
and most effectively saves lives.
So this is how we must preserve
the proper ordering of things,
and not, whatever happens, be subjected to a woman.
It's better, if needs must, to be defeated
by a man—for then at least we can't be said
to have been bettered by a female. 680

CHORUS-LEADER

You seem to us to speak good sense about these things,
if we've not lost our judgement through old age.

HAEMON

Father, the gods have planted in mankind
a thinking mind, the highest of all gifts.
I would not say your words are in the wrong,
and may I never want to;
but it may turn out as right in quite a different way.°
It is my place to keep good watch on your behalf
for all the things that anyone may say, or do, or criticize.
°You need to know the common people stand 690
in fear of you, in case they might say things
that you would not be pleased to hear.
For me, though, it's still possible to listen to
what's said in secret, and it's this:
°the city's filled with sorrow for this girl
because, most undeservedly of women,
she is due to die most horribly—
and yet for highly admirable deeds.
She is the one who did not let
her slaughtered brother lie unburied,
left for mutilation by wild dogs or crows—
so does she not deserve a crown of golden honour?
That's the sort of word that's darkly spread around. 700
For me there's nothing that's more precious, father,
than your prospering.
What lustre can there be more bright for children

than their father's flourishing with good repute?—
the same for fathers with their children.
So don't impose within yourself a single cast of mind:
that what you say, and nothing else, is always right.
For people who believe that they alone are sensible,
or they, and no one else, can speak—or feel—what's good,
when opened up they're found to be a blank.
There's nothing shameful for a man, however wise, 710
in learning yet, and not remaining over-rigid.
You see how when a tree beside a winter flood
bends pliantly, it stays with every twig intact,
while one that is unbending gets destroyed, uprooted.
And so too a mariner who keeps the sails stretched tight
and never slackens them capsizes,
and goes on his voyage with benches upside down.
Give way, then, and allow a change of heart.
If I, though younger, am allowed to show some sense,
I say that, while it would be great for men 720
to be infallible, since things are not inclined
to tip that way, it's good to learn
from those who offer good advice.

CHORUS-LEADER

My lord, if he says anything that's to the point,
it's only right for you to learn from him—
and he from you. Both sides have said good things.

CREON

Are men of our age to be tutored
in good sense by one as young as this?

HAEMON

Only in what is right. I may be young
but think of my achievements more than years.

CREON

And is it an achievement to exalt those causing trouble? 730

HAEMON

I wouldn't tell you to exalt those in the wrong.

CREON

But isn't that the plague this woman is afflicted by?

HAEMON
The common people here in Thebes do not agree.

CREON
And is the city telling me the way to rule?

HAEMON
Can you not see how juvenile that sounds?

CREON
Is ruling here my task—or someone else's?

HAEMON
It's no true city that belongs to just one man.

CREON
And is the city not considered as its ruler's realm?

HAEMON
Well, you would make the perfect monarch of a desert land.

CREON
It's clear this one is fighting on the woman's side. 740

HAEMON
If you're a woman—it's for you I am concerned.

CREON
By launching into quarrels with your father?

HAEMON
Only because I see you going badly wrong.

CREON
Do I go wrong if I respect my own authority?

HAEMON
It's no respect to trample over what is owed the gods.

CREON
Despicable, to be subjected to a woman!

HAEMON
At least you will not catch me crushed by wrong.

CREON
Well, everything you say is standing up for her.

HAEMON
For you as well, and me, and for the gods below. (749)

CREON

°Slave to a woman! Don't attempt to sweeten me. (756)

HAEMON

You want to speak, yet not to listen when you're spoken to?

CREON

You'll never have her, not while she is still alive. 750

HAEMON

In that case she shall die, and, dying, bring another down.

CREON

What? Are you really threatening so far?

HAEMON

What kind of threat is it to challenge empty thoughts?

CREON

You shall regret all this advice as your head's empty.

HAEMON

If you were not my father, I'd say you're the mindless one.

CREON

What's that? I swear by heaven above you'll not go
on and on insulting and abusing me unpunished.
(*to guards*) Bring out that abomination, 760
so that she can die now, here,
before her bridegroom's eyes.

HAEMON

Oh no, not me—don't ever think of that—
she shall not die in front of me.
And you shall never set your eyes on me again;
then you can rage with friends who want to stay with you.

Exit Haemon away from the direction of the city.

CHORUS-LEADER

He's gone, my lord, run off in fury.
Youthful hearts like his in pain can take things badly.

CREON

Well, let him act and think like someone more than man:
he won't be able to preserve those girls from death.

CHORUS-LEADER

But do you really mean to put them both to death? 770

CREON

No, not the one who had no hand in it. You're right.

CHORUS-LEADER

What kind of fate do you intend for her?

CREON

°I'll take her to a place that is untrod by human foot,
and there I'll close her up inside
a rocky cell dug underground.
I'll set out food sufficient to escape pollution,
so the city as a whole can still avoid miasma.
And there she can address her prayers to Hades,
who's the only god that she reveres,
and see if she can manage not to die.
Or else she will find finally that her obsession
with the underworld is labour spent in vain. 780

Exit Creon into the palace.

FOURTH CHORAL SONG

CHORUS

°Desire, never conquered in fight,
Desire, you invade every heart.°
The cheeks of a delicate girl
are where you encamp through the night;
you find your way over the seas,
and creep inside huts in the fields.
No god and no human escapes;
one who has you is utterly crazed. 790

You drag awry minds that are good,
and violently turn them to harm;
it is you who have stirred up this strife
between these two men of shared blood.
The nubile young bride with her gaze
stirs longing and lifts up the prize;
such passion defeats highest laws—°
Aphrodite invincibly plays. 800

SCENE 7 (LYRIC DIALOGUE)

°*Antigone is brought on by guards.*

CHORUS-LEADER

As I see this, even I am
swept beyond the laws' high order.
I can now restrain no longer
teardrops spilling as I witness
young Antigone here passing
to the room where all must sleep.

ANTIGONE

Here you see me, citizens
of my famous fatherland,
treading on my final way,
looking on my final sun,
never after this again. 810
Hades who lays all to sleep
takes me while I'm still alive
to the shore of Acheron;
cancelled from my wedding-day,
silenced from my marriage-song,
I shall lie with Acheron.

CHORUS-LEADER

Surely there's some fame and glory
in your going to the cavern
where the dead lie, yet not wasted
by diseases, nor dispatched by 820
warfare; but with independence
you alone of mortal women
pass on down to Hades, living.

ANTIGONE

°I have heard how Niobe,
who came to Thebes from Phrygia,
went back to a dreadful death.
Near the peak of Sipylus
she was cased about with stone,
gripping her as ivy creeps.

There the showers of rain and snow 830
falling ceaseless wear her smooth;
trickling tears drip from her brow,
constantly run down her cheeks.
She's most like to me indeed
as the god takes me to bed.

CHORUS-LEADER

°But she was divine, descended
from the race of gods, while we are
humans born of mortal parents.
All the same it makes your dying
shine to share a fate with godlike
equals, both in life and death.

ANTIGONE

I'm made a mockery!
By our ancestral gods,
why show contempt for me
in view and not yet gone? 840
O city, and you men,
rich citizens of Thebes,
and land of chariots
and Dirce's flowing streams,
you are my witnesses:
see how, unwept by friends,
condemned by what decrees,
I make my way towards
my bizarre burial,
my excavated cell,
not with the living, though, 850
nor with the dead below.

CHORUS-LEADER

Child, you pressed on to the verge of
daring, and then stumbled on the
mighty pedestal of justice,
paying for ancestral torment.

ANTIGONE

You've pressed my greatest wound:
my father's threefold pain,

and all our dynasty° 860
with its collective fate.
My mother's union was
disaster, coupling in
bed incestuous—
a father's mothering.
Such was my origin;
and back to them I pass,
child-sister settler,
unmarried and accursed.
And so your burial,° 870
my brother, has entailed
my death; your dying has
killed me alive as well.

CHORUS-LEADER

Your deed has a kind of rightness:
yet, for one in power, that power must
not be violated. You, it is your
wilful temper has destroyed you.

ANTIGONE

Without tears, without friends,
without wedding-chorus
I am led on to tread
this pathway before us.
I have to see no more
this sun's illumination; 880
I have no friend to mourn
my doom, no lamentation.

SCENE 8

Enter Creon abruptly from the palace, accompanied by guards.

CREON

For sure if chants and mourning
could hold death at bay,
then nobody would cease from them.
(*to guards*) Take her away at once,

and when you've wrapped her tight
inside the dug-out tomb, as I've instructed,
leave her there alone to see
if she would like to die, or live
incarcerated in a vault like that—
whichever way, our hands are clean
concerning this young woman.
What is sure is that she's going to be deprived 890
of dwelling here above.

ANTIGONE

°My tomb, my bridal chamber
and my deep-dug dwelling, my for-ever cell,
I go to you to join with my own people—
with so many of them down among the dead
admitted by Persephone.
And last of all of them I go, my ending far the worst,
before I've reached my proper share of life.
At least as I reach there I am sustained by hoping
I'll arrive as loving to my father,
and beloved for you, my mother,
and as loving towards you, dear brother;
since all of you, when you lay dead, I washed 900
and dressed and poured out
funeral offerings with my own hands.
And, Polynices, now it is for caring for your body
I'm receiving this reward.
And yet my act of honouring you
was in the eyes of thinking people good.
°[Because if children I was mother to,
or if a husband lay there dead and rotting,
I would not have taken on this labour
in defiance of the city's will.
What is the principle that I observe in saying this?
Suppose I had a husband who was dead,
there still could be another;
and I could still produce a child [910]
born of another man, if I had lost this one.
But, with my mother and my father

dead and down below, there is no way
another brother ever could be born.]
It's in accordance with this principle
I paid you this especial honour.
But Creon thinks that I did reckless wrong,
my dearest brother.
So now he's taken me by force, and leads me off,
me with no wedding-bed, no wedding-song,
without my share of marriage or of raising children.
But no, like this, bereft of friends, I make my way
alive into a dug-out cavern of the dead. 920
What justice of the gods have I transgressed?
But why continue looking to the gods?
What allies can I still invoke in prayer,
since I am singled out as wrong
for doing what was right?
Well, if this wins approval from the gods,
then through my suffering I'll come
to recognize my error:
but if it's these ones here who are in error,
may their pain turn out no less
than that unjustly visited on me.

CHORUS-LEADER
Still the same tempestuous storm-gusts
keep their hold upon her spirit. 930

CREON
That is why these warders will be
sorry they respond so slowly.

ANTIGONE
That command means death is very near. . . .

CREON
I have nothing else to offer:
this is what is going to happen.

The guards begin to take Antigone off.

ANTIGONE
O my city, and ancestral
Theban gods here, I am being

taken, and can stay no longer.
Look upon this, Theban elders— 940
me the last of this royal bloodline;
see what kind of man has made me
suffer, and for standing upright
holding on to what is right.

Exit Antigone, with guards, in the direction of the plain; Creon stays on.

FIFTH CHORAL SONG

CHORUS

°Danae had to endure
leaving the light of the skies,
and having her body immured
inside a cell bound with bronze sides.
She was constrained and secured
within a tomb-room, my child,
although she was noble, and cared
for Zeus-seed flowing with gold. 950
Fate has a dread kind of power,
such that there's nothing escapes,
not battle, nor wealth, nor high tower,
nor blackened sea-beaten ships.

°And Dionysus confined
Lycurgus to make him atone
for ill-tempered rage that defied
the god; shut in a prison of stone.
Slowly the froth of his rage
dripped till his madness was spent; 960
then he recognized how he had strayed
by insulting the god with mad taunts.
He tried to have women inspired
by the god restrained and suppressed,
and to quench Dionysian fire,
insulting the pipes of the Muse.

°And at Thracian Salmydessus
by the Black Sea's narrow strait, 970

there the cruel wife of Phineus
blackened her two step-sons' sight,
casting an accursed darkness
on their eyeballs' vengeful look,
mutilated, hands all bloodstained,
by her shuttle's pointed spike.

So they withered in their sorrow,
Cleopatra's blinded twins,
sons from her disastrous marriage. 980
She was born from ancient kings,°
nurtured in the North Wind's caverns,
flying proudly high and wild,
race of gods. And yet the age-old
Fates oppressed her too, my child.

SCENE 9

Tiresias has arrived unobtrusively from the city side, led by a servant.

TIRESIAS
Elders of Thebes, the two of us
have made our way here with one set of eyes—
the blind find out their pathway through their guide. 990

CREON
Well, old Tiresias, what is your news?

TIRESIAS
I shall instruct you. And you should obey the prophet.

CREON
I never have dissented from your judgement in the past.

TIRESIAS
And that is how you've kept this city safe on course.

CREON
I can confirm your value from experience.

TIRESIAS
Think hard: you're on the razor's edge.

CREON
What do you mean? I shudder at your tone.

TIRESIAS
You'll know from hearing what my art conveys.
Already as I took my seat upon the ancient place
for divination, where I have my refuge for all kinds of birds,° 1000
I could detect their unfamiliar sound
as they were screeching with unnatural frenzy.
I knew that they were ripping at each other with their talons
as the whirring of their wings was unmistakable.
Alarmed, I set about enquiry through burnt sacrifice,
and lit the tinder all around the altar;
but no flame took hold upon the offerings,
instead a murky liquid oozed out from the meat
upon the ash and made it smoke and hiss.
The gall was spattered, and the joints of meat 1010
lay bare without the fat which trickled off from them.
This is the way the rituals refused to yield
prophetic signs, as I discovered from this boy,
who is my leader just as I lead others.
And it is your will that makes the city sick like this,
because the altars and the sacrificial pits are clogged
with carrion torn by dogs and birds from off
the wretched body of the son of Oedipus.
And so the gods are not accepting prayers from us, 1020
nor sacrificial smoke from meat.
[Nor does the bird bescreech intelligible cries,
as they have feasted on the fat of human blood.]°
Please give hard thought to this, my son—
all human beings make mistakes sometimes;
and, when one does, it does not mean
he has to go on being foolish or unfortunate
if he sets out to remedy the trouble he has fallen in,
and does not stay immovable—
it's stubbornness that earns a verdict of stupidity.
So give way to the dead,
and don't keep stabbing one who's down.
What bravery is there in continuing to kill the dead? 1030

I mean good will to you when I say this;
It's a delight to learn from someone
who gives good advice if it brings gain.

CREON

Old man, you all of you let fly at me like archers
at a target—even with your prophecies.
I've long been bought and sold, negotiated, by your sort.
Pile up your gains, import electron coins
from Sardis,° gold from India, go on:
but, no, you shall not cloak that body
in the grave—not even if high Zeus's eagles 1040
want to snatch it up and bear the carrion to his throne,
not even then would I be scared by this miasma
into letting him have burial.
I don't believe a human has the power
to pass pollution to the gods.
Even the cleverest people, old Tiresias,
fall down in ugly ways when, out to make some gain,
they dress up ugly allegations in fine words.

TIRESIAS

That's bad. Does anybody know, or think . . .

CREON

Think what? What universal truth do you proclaim?

TIRESIAS

. . . how judgement is the greatest thing one can possess. 1050

CREON

Yes, just as much as foolish thinking does the greatest harm.

TIRESIAS

Well, that's the illness you're infected with.

CREON

I do not want to cast abuse back at the seer.

TIRESIAS

And yet you do when you condemn my prophecy as false.

CREON

Because all prophets are a money-grasping clan.

TIRESIAS
And tyrants also love corrupted ways of getting rich.

CREON
You realize it is your chief you are abusing?

TIRESIAS
I do. In fact it's thanks to me you've kept this city safe.

CREON
You are a clever prophet, but too fond of going wrong.

TIRESIAS
You'll stir me into saying things I'm keeping undisclosed. 1060

CREON
Go on, disclose! Don't speak for payment, though.

TIRESIAS
Is that what you believe I have been doing?

CREON
You'll never buy and sell my judgement, that's for sure.

TIRESIAS
°And you can be assured of this:
the sun shall not run many circuits more
before you shall have given one from your own blood,
a corpse in recompense for corpses.
This is to pay for thrusting down below
a human from this world above,
resettling a living spirit in the tomb,
whilst also keeping here above 1070
a corpse belonging to the gods below,
unportioned and unburied and unhallowed.
Yet these things are not for you to regulate,
nor for the gods above: they have been
violently displaced through your command.
So spirits of destruction, late to strike,
are waiting for you, powers of Hades and the gods;
so that you will be caught up in these selfsame wrongs.
Now look and see if I've been overlaid with silver—
this will be revealed through wear and tear
by men and women mourning in your house.°

°[And all the cities are becoming agitated [1080]
in resentment, where the dogs and beasts
and birds have swallowed bits of corpses,
spreading the polluted stink into the smoke from altars.]
So, since you've wounded me, in anger
I have aimed these arrows straight at you;
and you shall not be able to elude their sting.
(*to his servant*) My boy, now take me home,
and leave this one to vent his rage on younger men.
Then he may learn to cultivate a softer tone
and better cast of mind than he has now. 1090

Tiresias is led back towards the city.

CHORUS-LEADER
The man has gone, my lord, with terrifying prophecies.
Yet ever since my hair first turned to white from black,
I've never known him utter to our city
any warning that was false.

CREON
I know, and I am much perturbed.
While giving in is terrible,
to let my firm resolve come crashing down in ruins
would be so as well.

CHORUS-LEADER
Son of Menoeceus, you must summon wisdom.

CREON
What should I do then?
Tell me and I'll follow your advice.

CHORUS-LEADER
Go, let the girl free from her deep-dug cell, 1100
and organize the burial of thc body lying there.

CREON
You mean you recommend: that I give way?

CHORUS-LEADER
As quickly as you can, my lord.
The gods' reprisals cut short those who cling to wrong.

CREON

It's hard, but I must let go of my heart's resolve.
No good to fight against what has to be.

CHORUS-LEADER

Then do it, and don't delegate to others.

CREON

Yes, I shall go, just as I am.
Come on, come on, attendants far and wide,
bring heavy tools and hurry to that place in view. 1110
And I—now that my judgement has been overturned—
I shall be there myself, the one who closed her up,
to undo what's been done.
I'm coming to suspect that it is best
to go through life still keeping
to the long-established laws.

Exit Creon with attendants, towards the plain.

SIXTH CHORAL SONG

CHORUS

°O god of many names, we call on you,
the son of Theban maid and thunderer Zeus.°
You range through Italy,° and have your power
within Demeter's folds, hospitable 1120
Eleusis' holy shrine°—O Baccheus, come!
Your birthplace-home is Thebes, the mother-town
of bacchants, here beside Ismenus' flow
and dragon-meadow where the teeth were sown.

The torch's blazing light has sighted you
above the double crests of Delphi's heights,
where the Corycian nymphs go dancing, source
of the Castalian stream;° and ivy slopes 1130
of Nysa° by the coast grown thick with grapes—
all these domains of yours are sending you
to where your followers raise ritual shouts,
assembling to protect our Theban streets.

Thebes among all others
is the city you honour most,
here beside your mother
who was struck by the lightning bolt.°
Now her people suffer 1140
from attacks of malign disease,
so across Parnassus
or over the sounding seas
come to purify us,
and to grant us a pure release.

Cosmic chorus-leader
of the stars breathing fiery light,
and divine protector
as your worshippers sing by night,
great progeny of Zeus,
come, appear now—compassionate
epiphany—before us,
with your maenads who through the night 1150
dance and sing their chorus
as they celebrate your rite.°

SCENE 10

An attendant of Creon hurries on as messenger from the side of the plain.

MESSENGER

You citizens of Thebes,
I say there is no state of human life
that I would ever praise or criticize as fixed.
For constantly chance lifts and chance tips down
to make the fortunate unfortunate and back again;
so nobody can prophesy what stands as firm for humans. 1160
Take Creon.
He was enviable, so far as I could tell:
he'd saved this land of Thebes from enemies;
he'd taken over total sovereign power;
he flourished with fine children. . . .

And now that's gone, all gone.
For when delight has left a man deserted,
I would not count him as alive—
more like a corpse with breath.
Build up great wealth, go on, and live in regal style;
but if the joy has gone from this, 1170
I wouldn't give smoke's shadow for the rest,
not set against delight in life.

CHORUS-LEADER
What's this new grief you bring our royal house?

MESSENGER
They're dead. And it's the living are to blame.

CHORUS-LEADER
Who is the killer? Who the victim? Tell.

MESSENGER
It's Haemon dead, blood shed by his own blood.

CHORUS-LEADER
D'you mean his father did it? Or he killed himself?

MESSENGER
By his own hand, in fury at his father.

CHORUS-LEADER
Prophet, your words have turned out all too true!

MESSENGER
Therefore you should consider what to do.

CHORUS-LEADER
But here I see Eurydice,° poor wife of Creon. 1180
Is it chance she's coming out of doors,
or has she heard about her son?

Eurydice has entered from the palace door.

EURYDICE
Good citizens, I heard some talk as I was coming out
to go and supplicate Athena with my prayers.
I was unfastening the door-bolts when some news
of troubles for this household reached my ears,

so that I fainted back into my women's arms.
Yet tell again whatever that news was— 1190
I'm well experienced in grief.°

MESSENGER

I was right there, dear mistress,
and I'll not pass over any word of truth.
What would be the point of reassuring you
when later I'll be seen to have been lying?
Truth is always best.
I attended on your husband to the far edge of the plain,
to where the corpse of Polynices,
torn about by dogs, unpitied, lay.
With prayers to Hecate and Hades 1200
to be kind and hold their anger back,
we washed him with pure water,
and then burnt his last remains
upon a pyre of new-cut brushwood.
When we'd heaped his mound of native earth,
we moved towards the bridal-chamber
of the maiden with its bed of rock.
From far away we heard loud crying sounds
that echoed round that cursèd portico,
and went to warn our master Creon.
As he came nearer, incoherent cries of grief 1210
engulfed him, and he cried aloud in anguish:
'Ah, am I to be the prophet then?
Am I upon the most disastrous path I've ever trod?
That's my son's voice that's greeting me.
Come, servants, hurry close and peer
into the tomb—go through the hole there
where the wall of stones has been torn down.°
See if I'm right to recognize that voice as Haemon's,
or if I am deluded by the gods.'
So following our master's anxious words,
we went and looked. 1220
There in the furthest corner of the tomb we saw her,
hanging from a fastened noose of linen cloth.
And him beside, embracing her around the waist,

lamenting for his marriage-partner killed
and gone below, and for his father's actions,
and his own unhappy union.
When Creon saw, he went towards him
calling in a dreadful, pleading tone:
'O no, what have you done?
What were you thinking?
What is it has so maddened you?
Come out, my son, I beg of you.' 1230
His son just glared at him, wild-eyed,
and, making no reply, spat in his face;
then drew his two-edged sword,
but, as his father hurried to escape,
he missed his blow.
And there and then the poor boy, angry with himself,
hard braced his body on the blade,
and plunged it half its length into his side.
Then, still alive, he took the woman in his arms
and clung to her; with gasps he showered spurts
of crimson blood upon her pallid cheek.
His body lies enfolded with her body, 1240
so the poor man has fulfilled his wedding rites
below in Hades' house.
He's surely demonstrated how bad thinking
is for humans far the worst of faults.

°*Eurydice goes indoors.*

CHORUS-LEADER

What do you make of this? The lady has gone back
indoors without a word of any kind.

MESSENGER

I am surprised as well. My hope is that,
on hearing of her son's last agonies,
she did not want to make a mournful noise in public,
but indoors will have her maids raise cries
of lamentation for this family grief.
She has the sense to keep clear of committing wrong. 1250

CHORUS-LEADER

I'm not so sure. To me excessive silence
seems as serious as too much crying out aloud.

MESSENGER

I'll find out if she's holding back some hidden impulse
by going in myself. You're right
that extreme silence may be ominous.

Messenger goes inside, as Creon approaches from the direction of the plain with the body of Haemon.

SCENE II (LYRIC DIALOGUE)

CHORUS-LEADER

°Here the king himself is coming,
carrying a clear reminder,
to be honest, of his downfall—
his and no one else's error. 1260

CREON

Mistakes of my ill-judged judgement
inflexible, deathwards tending!
You see kindred killed and killer,
disaster of my mis-thinking.
(*cry of distress, then to the dead Haemon*)
You lie dead, your young life ended
through my, not your, ill thinking.

CHORUS-LEADER

Too late, it seems, you've understood what's right. 1270

CREON

Yes, I have learnt from my mistakes.
Back then a god beat on my head with heavy blows,
and threw me far off course on savage tracks,
and so has overturned and trampled on my joys.
Such pain on pain weighs down our human ways.

The messenger-attendant re-enters from the house.

MESSENGER

You have, my lord, one burden and you will get more.
The one you carry in your arms,
and soon you shall set eyes upon
the other sorrow in your house. 1280

CREON

What can there be that's yet more terrible to add?

MESSENGER

Your wife, true mother of this corpse,
lies dead from stabs just dealt.

CREON

O harbour of death, undraining,
why more and more, why destroy me?
Bad-news-bringer, what new sorrow?
You crush a man down already.
(*cry of distress*)
What's this increased disaster— 1290
my wife heaped on the slaughter?

°*The body of Eurydice is brought out.*

MESSENGER

See for yourself; her body is no more indoors.

CREON

Here is a second soul-destroying sight.
Can there, can there be any further doom in wait?
It was just now my arms took up my son,
and here I see her lying dead before my feet.
Unhappy mother and poor child, both gone. 1300

MESSENGER

Before the altar <she took up a sword
and pierced herself> upon its sharpened point.°
As darkness fell upon her eyes,
she cried out for the glorious fate
of Megareus,° the son who died before,
and then for Haemon here;
and with her dying breaths she sang the litany
of your wrong deeds that killed your child.

CREON

I'm whirled aloft with dread.
Why doesn't somebody
take up a sharp-edged blade
and strike me fatally?
I'm steeped in bitter pain,
infused with misery. 1310

MESSENGER

Indeed this woman here, now dead,
denounced you for this death and those before.

CREON

How was it that she brought about her end?

MESSENGER

When she had heard her son's appalling fate,
with her own hand she stabbed deep in herself.

CREON

The blame for this cannot be pinned
on someone else. I am the one.
For I killed you, yes you I killed—
truth must be told. My servants, take, 1320
take me to far away, and quick,
the man who is no more alive
than somebody who does not breathe.

CHORUS-LEADER

That's well advised, if there is any good in such bad times.
Best to be brief when troubles strew the way.

CREON

Please come, O let it come,
the finest fate for me,
far best, my final day. 1330
O let it come, please come,
so that I never see
another shining day.

CHORUS-LEADER

°That is the future: it's the present calls for action.
Matters must be left to those who should take care of them.

CREON

But I have prayed for everything that I desire.

CHORUS-LEADER

Then pray no more. There's no release for humans
from events that have to be.

CREON

Please take away this empty man,
who did not mean to kill you, son, 1340
and you as well, my wife, my own.
I don't know where to point my sight,
nor where to lean. For every deed
I take in hand skews off from straight.
Cruel fate has swooped down on my head.

Attendants take Creon and the two bodies indoors.

CHORUS

Wisdom is the first prescription
for good living: never rashly
spurn the gods. Disdainful language 1350
gets repaid with painful lashes,
teaching us in old age wisdom.

The chorus go off in the direction of the city.

DEIANEIRA

INTRODUCTION TO *DEIANEIRA*

Note on the title

THE ancient title of this play was *Trachiniai*, taken from the chorus which is made up of women from Trachis, the town where it is set. Heracles' family have taken refuge there after his exclusion from other places because of his past acts of violence. Trachis (see the map) was not a place of great mythical or political importance;[1] and its chief significance for this tragedy is that it is close to the massif of Mount Oeta (Greek *Oite*) where Heracles' funeral pyre was famously located. The usual modern titles *Women of Trachis* or *Trachinian Women* have no particular resonances, and may be felt, indeed, to be rather off-putting because of their obscurity. So I have felt justified in seeking for a more appealing alternative.

I have settled on *Deianeira.* It is true that she too is relatively little-known, and that she has a slightly esoteric-sounding name, but since she is the most interesting character, and dominates three-quarters of the play—and in view of its place in this volume of the three 'female' tragedies of Sophocles—*Deianeira* calls for the spotlight. I had also considered *The Wife of Heracles*, *The Death of Heracles*, and even *The Shirt of Nessus*,[2] but the title *Deianeira* reflects the way that, while she herself defines her role as the hero's spouse, she is ultimately a more powerful tragic figure than he is.

Why an Underrated Tragedy?

There were many stories current before Sophocles' play about the great super-hero Heracles, especially about his 'labours' (which were eventually canonized into twelve). The stories extended from his strangling snakes in his cradle, via many places including Troy and the island of the Hesperides, to his being burnt on a bonfire on Mount

[1] It survives in modern times as the name of a halt on the Thessaloniki to Athens railway line!

[2] The use of 'shirt' for this robe is best known from Shakespeare's *Antony and Cleopatra*, where Antony, facing humiliating defeat, complains 'The shirt of Nessus is upon me'.

Oeta as the only way to put an end to the agony caused by the robe (or 'shirt') poisoned with the blood of Nessus. They told, among many other exploits, of how in a fit of madness he killed his wife Megara and their children at Thebes; how he fought the river-god Achelous to win the hand of Deianeira; and how he sacked the city of Oechalia (location uncertain) to obtain the beautiful Iole. It was a life-story of such larger-than-life derring-do, so voracious, so grotesque at times, that it made Heracles unsuitable to be an archetypal figure for tragedy,[3] and, indeed, made him more familiar on the comic stage.

This ambivalence about the 'seriousness' of Heracles may be part of the reason for the way that *Deianeira* has been the least known of Sophocles' seven surviving plays, and one of the two least performed.[4] I strongly believe that it deserves to be better appreciated. First, Sophocles sets the story in a disturbingly unfamiliar borderland between a primeval world of monsters and 'our' world of settled society. River-gods, hydras, Centaurs, and other mythical creatures are synchronous with family life, marital loyalty, human rationality, understanding, and misunderstanding. Heracles moves between both worlds, but they are ultimately irreconcilable: his life as the monster-slaying hero destroys his family life, and in the end destroys himself. It is telling that Heracles and Deianeira are never on stage together: they stand for worlds that can never be merged. Deianeira presents the anxieties of wifehood and motherhood, threatened by the intrusion of her husband's lust for a younger woman's body. Her conflicts and confusions are human, and all too familiar for ordinary people. Heracles, on the contrary, is the son of Zeus, and has spent his life confronting foes, winning trophies, and possessing women. Along with his prowess go pride, anger, and lust. In the end he lives and dies bound up in a world of monstrous strength.

Why has this play, nonetheless, been relatively overlooked? Sophocles has seldom been explicitly criticized in the way that Euripides has been, and so working out negative responses has to be to some extent guesswork. Some readers have found the portrayal of Heracles overblown and even un-human. He entirely dominates the last quarter of the play, and spends much of this on repeatedly complaining of the agonies that he is suffering, and on railing against his unmerited

[3] Euripides nonetheless creates a tragic figure in his *Heracles*.

[4] The other is *Aias*.

humiliation. He devotes a very long speech (1046–1110) to his mighty deeds in the past, now bought down by a mere woman. And when he finds out about the mistaken good intentions and death of Deianeira, he shows no interest or regret whatsoever. Instead he goes on to pressure his loyal son, Hyllus, to agree to take on Iole as his wife, even though she has proved to be, however innocently, his mother's downfall. Heracles insists, with characteristic insensitivity, that this is only a 'small' demand (1217, 1229).

So it is hard to feel much 'sympathy' for this Heracles. But we should put in the other scale that he is not portrayed as a mere brute, and that this is not an everyday story of sordid marital infidelity. This son of Zeus is no ordinary man, and it might be claimed that he should not be judged by ordinary human standards. He is fuelled by more-than-human passions; and he makes no pretence to be super-virtuous. And in the end is he even mortal? Does he die like everyone else? The play leaves this question tantalizingly open, and the issue will be explored more fully on pages 73-5 below. Whatever the colouring of the ending of the play, Heracles is presented as, for all his flaws, indisputably the 'greatest' human who has ever lived—at least by the traditional measures of heroic greatness. As Hyllus says in the last words that Deianeira hears as she leaves the scene to kill herself (811–12):

> You've killed the greatest man of all upon the earth,
> whose like we shall not see again.

In any case it is Deianeira, not Heracles, who dominates the first three-quarters of the play. She is deeply human, far from superhuman, and is open about her frailties. Indeed, she is, it may be claimed, a highly sympathetic, almost 'modern', individual. In the past, however, some readers and critics have been at least somewhat negative towards her, and this disapproval may have been a factor in the undervaluing of the play as a whole. She has been seen as a selfish, over-possessive woman: there is, after all, nothing so unusual (they say) about a powerful man taking a mistress—or even several. Such a man cannot be expected to be satisfied by an ageing spouse. Indeed Deianeira herself seems to acknowledge as much (459–63):

> Heracles has been to bed
> with many, many women, hasn't he?
> And yet not one of them has had to face

> abuse or blame from me.
> Nor shall this one, not even if he's utterly
> consumed in his desire for her.

And the herald Lichas praises this worldly attitude (472–3):[5]

> I see, dear mistress, that you think
> in human terms, and not inflexibly.

Some critics have maintained that she is in fact driven by sexual jealousy all along, and that this apparent complaisance is a calculating deceit. That would make her a crafty manipulative female, however understandable. There is, however, no hint at all in the text that Deianeira is being deliberately deceitful: rather she is trying to persuade herself that she should adopt the worldly attitude of males to their sexual appetites. What she has not reckoned with, and what she does not recognize until she has gone indoors into her house, is that this new sexual rival is no secret mistress,[6] but will be there sharing her household space. As Deianeira envisages it (539–40):

> And now the two of us shall lie
> beneath a single coverlet,
> and wait to see which one he will embrace.

It is important, then, and surely 'sympathetic' that what Deianeira cannot stomach is not the idea that Heracles should have bedded other women, but that he intends to do so in her own house, the house she has so loyally kept for him.

The other complaint that has been raised against Deianeira is that she is allegedly stupid. She shows herself as half-aware that sending her husband a love-potion (smeared on cloth) is dubious behaviour for a respectable woman (582–6):

> I hope that I may never know or learn dark practices;
> and I hate women who experiment with them:
> but if I can in some way make this potion
> work on Heracles with charms that will outbid
> this girl, well then, the process has been set.

[5] See also lines 627–9.

[6] This was, according to the Old Man's report what Heracles had initially wanted (360): 'when he could not persuade her father | to give up the girl to be his secret mistress. . . .'

Surely, it is complained, she should have realized sooner that a favour offered by the dying Centaur Nessus was bound to be malicious. But, since Nessus was dying because of his erotic desire for her, might he not be doing her a sexual favour in recognition of this? She may fairly be accused of being naïve, and of being susceptible to jealousy and to protectiveness for her own status, but these are not traits to be bluntly condemned. On the contrary, to the sensibilities of the twenty-first century at least, her attitude is understandable and forgivable.

Deianeira, Domesticity, and Monstrosity

It is, indeed, Deianeira's relationship with the man of power and his world that is central to the case for the re-evaluation of the play in the twenty-first century. Heracles did not marry her for the beauty of her soul, but for the beauty of her body. He did not fight the river-god Achelous to rescue a damsel in distress, but so that he could have her in his bed. Her beauty is her danger; as she says (24–5):

> I sat there petrified with dread
> that my own beauty might result in agony for me.

Then, less than a day's travel away from Achelous, it is again her beauty that brings conflict: the Centaur Nessus could not resist its allure, and he pays with his life.

When the play begins it has been a good many years (at least twenty) that Deianeira has kept Heracles' household, borne him children, and worried about his welfare. Most of the time he has been away—as she vividly puts it (31–2):

> Yes, we have children, but he—
> like some farmer with an isolated plot of land—
> devotes attention to them only at the time
> of sowing and of harvest.

Over these years Heracles may well have had other women, but none is named or specified.[7] It is implied that Iole, the daughter of Eurytus of Oechalia, is the first that he has actually brought back home. In the version of the story, as initially given by his agent Lichas (254 ff.), the

[7] He has recently spent a year as a slave to the Lydian queen Omphale, but it is not made clear whether or not he had to serve her in bed.

reason why Heracles sacked Oechalia, killing its men and enslaving its women, was that he had been outrageously insulted by Eurytus. Later Lichas admits that it was really because of Iole. Furthermore, it seems that Heracles is proud of this. The old man repeats what he heard Lichas say (351–5):

> I heard this herald say in front of lots of witnesses
> that it was all because of this young woman
> Heracles destroyed Eurytus and his citadel Oechalia.
> And Eros was the only god who lured him to this war. . . .

Once Heracles has come back, he makes no allusion to this in his agony, and he does not admit to any fault. He shows no remorse about the fate of Deianeira, and unashamedly makes Hyllus take his place in Iole's bed (1225–7):

> Do not let any other man but you possess her,
> who has lain with me,
> her body pressed to mine.

So Iole also is a victim of Heracles' overmastering sex-drive. She is evidently young and beautiful, and, when she sees her, Deianeira speculates on her life-story (307–9):

> Poor creature, who are you among these girls?
> Unmarried? Or have you a child? (*no response*)
> Your manner seems to say you're not experienced
> in all these things. . . .

Later, however, when the truth has come out, she speaks in very different terms (536–40):

> I have, you see, let in a girl—
> and yet no more a simple girl, I think,
> a fully harnessed woman—
> I've taken her on board,
> the way a merchant stows a cargo;
> but these goods will wreck my peace of mind.
> And now the two of us shall lie
> beneath a single coverlet,
> and wait to see which one he will embrace.

Yet, for all her jealousy, she was intuitively right to feel an affinity: they both share in Heracles' bed as a consequence of their beauty, and through his violent ways of getting the woman he wants.

All the same, no one expressly condemns Heracles, except for once: Deianeira in the lines that immediately follow those just quoted (540–2):

> Is this the kind of payment
> that the so-called good and trusty Heracles
> has sent me in return for caring for his house
> through such a stretch of time?

His hyper-libido is treated as all part of the strong-man package—it is not hard to think of modern parallels! What is so interesting about Deianeira is that she is not portrayed as a mere passive victim. She struggles with the inequity of her world. At the same time she is not a ruthless avenger either (no Clytemnestra or Medea). She has devoted her life to the house and bed of Heracles, and in a sense she has come to love them, as the sympathy of the women of the chorus reflects, and as is made clear when she kills herself on the marital bed.

Is there some sense, then, in which Heracles gets the suffering that he deserves? Is he punished, even, for his excesses? After all, despite all his mighty deeds, and even though Zeus is his father, he does in the end meet an agonizing death. Is this a kind of corollary of his violent and libidinous life—he who lives by testosterone shall die by testosterone? This may sound neat, but there is something more complicated going on; and this raises the whole issue of the ending of the play.

Heracles and the Pyre on Mount Oeta

By the time of Sophocles there were two incompatible accounts of what happened to Heracles after the end of his life. One had him down in Hades along with all other mortals—'even Heracles . . .'. Other versions, however, took him up to Olympus where he enjoyed an afterlife of immortal privilege, even sharing his bed with Hebe, the goddess who personified the bloom of youth. And these stories of his ascension to the realm of the gods were often associated with his funeral pyre on Mount Oeta. The story was that he was fetched out of the flames by a divine chariot, and carried, shining in his armour, up into the sky.[8] That pyre is precisely where he is about to be taken at the end of our play.

[8] This is explicitly alluded to by the chorus at Sophocles' *Philoctetes* lines 726–9.

There was a well-known cult site there on Oeta, where annual sacrifices were made, adding to the huge ash-pile that built up over the years.[9] It seems very likely that Sophocles' audience—or at least most of them—will have been aware of this cult, and of its association with Heracles' translation to a hedonistic afterlife. So there can be little doubt that this is in some way hinted at the end of *Deianeira*. There is nothing explicit or assured, but the possibility must be there. Would that mean, though, that, far from being in any way punished, Heracles is in fact rewarded in the end?

While this is a disputed issue, it seems most plausible to take it that the play ends on an uncertain note. Has Zeus abandoned his far-from-perfect son to an appropriately extreme death? Or does the very name of Oeta cast something of a golden glow from beyond the conclusion? How is one to know? The difficulty of attaining knowledge, and the further difficulties that knowledge can bring, have in fact been a recurrent motif of the play. At one point, when trying to elicit the truth from Lichas, Deianeira asks (459) 'What is so terrible in knowing?'. The play goes on to show, all too tellingly, how terrible things may indeed flow from knowing. At the same time, it is arguably a fundamental human drive to want to know. It might, indeed, be maintained that it is a central concern in tragedy of all eras that humans have a need to know. And yet that knowledge can prove to be far from a blessing; it may, on the contrary, lead to terrible consequences.

And how secure is whatever knowledge we can grasp? How complete is it? What remains still obscured? Such uncertainty is one reason why oracles and prophecies play such a large part in some Greek tragedies, including *Deianeira*. Oracles give a partial picture of the truth, but they are at the same time open to misunderstandings and uncertainties. Thus an oracle evoked at several junctures in this play said that after a certain time Heracles would be at last released from his labours. This is taken to mean that he will enjoy a long life of ease; but, as the chorus are the first to see clearly, there is another way of fulfilling this prediction (827–30):

> Time has steered that to its port
> truly as it said:

[9] This has been located archaeologically. It is not at the highest point (2150 m. above sea-level), but at a more accessible spot on the southern side at about 1500 m., not far from the modern village of Pavliani.

for how could someone take on more
labours if they're dead?

And Heracles himself comes to see this (1169–73):

I thought this meant that I should go on happily,
but what it meant was I should die—
because no troubles are imposed upon the dead.

It is after this realization that he gives instructions about being taken to a pyre on Oeta. Even then, though, there is no indication that he knows what that will bring apart from the end of his agony. And the audience is left not knowing either.

The possibility of a blessed future has to be measured within the context of the way that Sophocles actually closes the play. It has to be set side-by-side with the agonies and dilemmas of the final scenes, summed up in Hyllus' last lines before the funerial procession sets off. His last response[10] takes the form of a rebuke against the gods, and Zeus in particular, and is expressed in extraordinarily fierce terms (1264–72):

Come, my comrades, lift his body.
Grant to me your deepest fellow-
feeling: but condemn the gods for
deepest lack of any feeling.
They get children and are famed as
fathers, yet look down indifferent
on such dreadful scenes of suffering.
No one can foresee the future,
but this present shows us right for
pity, yet shows them as shameful.[11]

Those lines give the human perspective. Even if there is an apotheosis in store, the present human suffering is grim and inexplicable. And this should not be diluted by inappropriate associations with religious

[10] It is disputed who says the very closing lines at 1275–9, but, as argued in the note on them, it is improbable that it was Hyllus.

[11] This passage caught the eye of Thomas Hardy. In his hugely ambitious, if flawed, epic-drama, *The Dynasts*, he has one of his chorus-like Spirits, the Spirit of the Pities, say: 'A life there was | Among these self-same frail ones—Sophocles— | Who visioned it too clearly, even the while | He dubbed the Will "the gods". Truly said he | "Such great injustice to their own creation | Burdens the time with mournfulness for us, | And for themselves with shame."'

notions of martyrdom or of Paradise. According to these (to put it crudely) an afterlife of eternal blessings for those who have merited it redeems the suffering of this brief mortal life. Greek tragedy does not admit any such evasions of the immediacy of human suffering; it never looks over the shoulder of this life, so to speak, at the party which is being enjoyed in the next room, the afterlife. In other words the prospect, left uncertain in any case, of Heracles' immortality does not *redeem* his terrible agony in the robe of Nessus. Nor does it do anything to lighten or excuse the sufferings of the women who have been dragged down by his sexual voracity. A more comfortable ending would have made this a less great play.

DEIANEIRA

LIST OF CHARACTERS

DEIANEIRA, daughter of Oeneus of Pleuron; the wife of Heracles, and now living at Trachis

OLD SERVING WOMAN, household slave woman, close to Deianeira

HYLLUS, a son of Deianeira and Heracles

OLD MAN, a lively local (often known as 'Messenger')

LICHAS, herald, high-status personal assistant to Heracles

IOLE (silent), daughter of Eurytus of Oechalia, captured by Heracles to be his lover

OLD ATTENDANT, in charge of those looking after the suffering Heracles, possibly some kind of doctor

CHORUS of young women of the town of Trachis

Place: in front of the house in Trachis where the family of Heracles has settled. One of the side-directions goes to the civic areas of the town, and beyond that to the shore and overseas. The other goes towards Mount Oeta and is only used at the very end of the play.

SCENE I (PROLOGUE)

Deianeira emerges from the house, with an old serving woman in attendance.

DEIANEIRA

There is an age-old saying that
you cannot gauge a human life
as being either good or bad
before a person dies.
But I know well enough, before I ever come near death,
that mine is miserable and burdensome.
While still within my father's house in Pleuron
I—the worst for any female in Aetolia—was forced
to face a dreadful wedding-match.
I had a river-god, the Achelous,° wooing me.
He came to ask my father for my hand 10
in triple form: sometimes a full-grown bull,
sometimes a coiling serpent,
and sometimes a human torso with a bull below;
and streams of water tumbled down his shaggy beard.°
Confronted with a bridegroom such as this
I prayed and prayed that I might die
before I ever had to lie down in that bed of his.
But just in time, and much to my delight,
great Heracles arrived,
the son of Zeus and Alcmene;°
who took this creature on in battle and delivered me. 20
I could not tell you how the fighting went—
though one who watched it without fear might know—
but as for me, I sat there petrified with dread
that my own beauty might result in agony for me.
Eventually Zeus concluded matters happily—
if happily it was. . . .
For ever since I was awarded to the bed of Heracles,
I've lived with fear forever growing out of fear
in my concern for him.
One night brings one anxiety, 30

and then the next displaces it.
Yes, we have children, but he—
like some farmer with an isolated plot of land—
devotes attention to them only at the time
of sowing and of harvest.
That's the way of life that brings my husband home
only to send him off again—at somebody's command.°
And now that he has overcome these labours
I'm especially afraid.
For ever since he killed great Iphitus°
we have been living here displaced in Trachis;°
but for him . . . nobody knows where he has gone. 40
I only know that he has left me aching
with a bitter longing.
I am almost sure he's in distress,
because it's no short time, but fully fifteen months,
we've had no message sent.
And something bad has happened:
that's the meaning of the written tablet°
that he left me with. I keep on praying to the gods
that that did not spell grief.

OLD SERVING WOMAN

(*stepping forward*) My mistress Deianeira,
I have often watched your bitter sorrows, 50
weeping for how Heracles has gone away.
If it is ever justified for slaves to give advice
to those free-born, now is the time I should speak out:
since you have got a clutch of sons,°
why don't you send one off to find out news?
Hyllus would be the most appropriate,
if he cares for his father's being well regarded.

Hyllus approaches in haste from the 'local' side.

And here he is, returning quickly home—
so if you think that my advice is to the point,
this is your chance to urge him on. 60

DEIANEIRA

(*to Hyllus*) My son, my boy, some good ideas may come

from those of lowly birth—this woman here's a slave,
yet what she says is worthy of one free.

HYLLUS

What do you mean? Instruct me, mother, if you can.

DEIANEIRA

That when your father's been so long away,
it's shameful you've not tried to find out where he is.

HYLLUS

But I already know—at least if we can trust what's said.

DEIANEIRA

What have you heard of where he is?

HYLLUS

He had to spend the whole of this past year
as servant to a Lydian lady.° 70

DEIANEIRA

If he put up with that, no news will seem incredible.

HYLLUS

But now I hear he's been released from there.

DEIANEIRA

Where is he said to be these days, alive or dead?

HYLLUS

They say he's mounting an attack against
Eurytus' city in Euboea°—or he's going to.

DEIANEIRA

Are you aware, my son, that he has left me
with an oracle about this very land?

HYLLUS

What sort of message, mother? I've not heard of this.

DEIANEIRA

That either he is going to meet the ending of his life,
or else that, after taking on this contest, 80
he shall spend the rest of all his days at peace.°
So since his fate is poised at such a tipping-point,
you ought to go and work along with him,
because if he survives then we shall too—

or else with him we're lost.
[or else we go down with your father's death.°]

HYLLUS
Then, mother, I shall go.
If I had known the burden of these prophecies,
I would have joined with him before.
But up till now my father's usual success
allowed us not to worry or to fear too much.
But now I am aware of this, I'll do the best I can 90
to find out all the truth about these things.

DEIANEIRA
Go then, my son. To learn of good success,
if only late, delivers gain.

Hyllus sets off in the 'abroad' direction; Deianeira stays; the chorus comes on from the same side.

FIRST CHORAL SONG (PARODOS)

CHORUS
°The glimmering night gives birth to you
as she is killed,
and puts you back to sleep in turn
with blaze of gold—
O Sun! Now tell me this one thing,
where's Heracles,
Alcmena's son, just where is he?
Tell, dazzling blaze!
Could he be in the east beside
the Black Sea strait:° 100
or west between the pillared continents?
Say, lord of sight!

For Deianeira's heart, we know,
has bled and bled
with unrelenting, longing pain,
like some sad bird.
She cannot close her yearning eyes,
with tears all dried,

for anxious fear about her man,
so far abroad.
She pines upon her fretful bed
without its mate, 110
and in her misery forebodes
some dreadful fate.

°As on the open sea the waves
come on and on increasing
before the stormy winds from south
or north with blasts unceasing:
like that the heaving ocean swell
of Heracles' life-toiling
obscures him sometimes down in troughs,
at others lifts his glory.
And yet some god looks after him,
and keeps him safe from tripping, 120
ensuring that he stays above,
where Hades cannot trap him.

With deference, I do not join
in your way of despairing,
since, Deianeira, my advice
is: do not keep on wearing
down hopeful thoughts in anxious gloom.
For Zeus the all-achieving
has not bestowed a pain-free life
upon our mortal being;
no, joy and sorrow come around
for humans in a cycle, 130
as the Great Bear wheels its path
in a revolving circle.

Nothing stays for life in one condition—
not the glimmering night, nor grim perdition,
nor great riches—since upon a sudden
things shift over to another person
to be glad and then ungladdened.
So don't push this hope away abandoned:
Zeus is never careless of his children. 140

SCENE 2

DEIANEIRA

Presumably you've heard of my distress,
yet may you never come to know my depth of agony,
but stay, as now, without experience.
The sapling of young life is raised
in its own nursery, protected
from the heat and rain and lashing winds;
and so it grows contented with delight,
until the time when it is called a wife and not a girl.
Then she assumes her share of night-time worry,
filled with fear about her husband or her children. 150
Anyone like that could understand
from her own case the ills I'm burdened with.
I have lamented over many troubles, then;
but there is one, unknown before,
which I should tell you of.
When Heracles was setting off on this last journey,
he left here at home a solemn tablet
all inscribed with writing.
He never had before, as he left on his labours,
laid down matters to me in this way,
but always went as set on action not on death. 160
This time, like one who lives no more, he told me
what I ought to take as property by marriage,
and what portions of ancestral land
should be allotted to his sons.
And he set down a certain time—
that is, when he had been away for fifteen months—
when he was either bound to die,
or else, surviving through that crisis-time,
should spend his life-span free of further pain.
He said this was determined by the gods
to be the outcome of the Heraclean labours, 170
as once spoken by the ancient oak-tree
of Dodona through the pair of Doves.°
The moment for these things to be fulfilled

is now, this present time exactly.
That, dear friends, is why, when I am pleasantly asleep,
I start awake in terrified alarm,
for fear I shall be left bereaved,
the widow of the greatest man of all.

°*The old man approaches from the 'abroad' direction.*

CHORUS-LEADER

Don't say such things, since I can see a man approaching,
garlanded like one with joyful things to tell.

OLD MAN

My lady Deianeira, I shall be the first 180
to bring the news that frees you from anxiety.
For Heracles is here, alive:
triumphant from his wars he's bringing home
the choicest offerings for our local gods.°

DEIANEIRA

What's this you're telling me, old man?

OLD MAN

Your celebrated husband shall be soon arriving
at your house, all glowing with the strength of victory.

DEIANEIRA

Who have you heard this from? A local or a stranger?

OLD MAN

The herald Lichas is regaling a whole crowd
down in the Oxen Mead.° When I heard him,
I hurried off to be first to bring you news, 190
and so obtain your favour and reward.

DEIANEIRA

Why's he not here himself, if he's so fortunate?

OLD MAN

He cannot make much headway, mistress,
since the folk of Malis° are surrounding him,
and asking questions, stopping him from moving on.
Each longs to know and will not let him go
until they've heard their fill—

so they do what they want, while he can not.
But you shall soon be seeing him direct.

DEIANEIRA

O Zeus, high lord of Oeta's uncropped meadow-grass,° 200
you have at long last granted us this joy!
Now, women, raise your cry, both those indoors
and you outside the gate, as we enjoy the light
beyond our hopes that's glowing with this news.

CHORUS (*singing*)

°Let the marriageable women
halloo° the household chorus;
let the men sing loud to honour
Apollo who cares for us.
Come, you girls, and chant the paean 210
to Artemis to save us—
torch-god, hunter of wild deer—
joined by the Nymphs our neighbours.
See me stirred up by the *aulos*,°
O you my spirit's master;
see how Dionysian ivy
can set me whirling faster! 220

Lichas and a band of captive women approach; they include Iole among them.

(*to Deianeira*) Look on happily, dear mistress,
io paian, I sing you.
See, these things are near approaching
and coming clear in view.

DEIANEIRA

I do see them, dear women, as my watchful eye
had noted this procession coming.

Lichas and company have by now arrived.

I bid you welcome, herald, now you have appeared—
assuming that you bring us welcome news.

LICHAS

We're glad to be here, and to hear

your greeting, lady, fitting the achievement. 230
For when a man does well, it's only right
for him to have the benefit of words of praise.

DEIANEIRA

Dear friend, first tell me what I firstly want to know:
am I to welcome Heracles back home alive?

LICHAS

He was alive, when I last left him,
strong and in the best of health.

DEIANEIRA

Where was this? In our homeland or some foreign place?

LICHAS

There is a headland in Euboea, where he's marking out
an altar to present first offerings to Zeus of Caeneum.°

DEIANEIRA

To carry out some vow? Or following some oracle?

LICHAS

A vow he made when he was ravaging the country 240
of these women that you see before you.°

DEIANEIRA

And who are they? And whose are they?
If I'm not wrong about their state, they should be pitied.

LICHAS

When he had sacked Eurytus' city,
Heracles selected them,
possessions for himself and for the gods.

DEIANEIRA

And was it to attack this city he was gone
for such an unforeseen long time?

LICHAS

Not only that, because for much of it
he was, as he admits, detained in Lydia,
not free but purchased as a slave.
And yet you should not disapprove, dear lady: 250
since it's clear that Zeus made sure this came about.
[He was sold off to Omphale, the foreign queen,
to serve a whole year long, as he himself admits.°]

He was so stung by this humiliation
that he bound himself by oath
that he would one day make the man
who had subjected him to this a slave,
and take his wife and child° as well.
And he stood by his word: once he was purified,
he raised a foreign army and attacked
the city of Eurytus, on the grounds that he alone 260
had been the man to blame for this disgrace.°
It was like this. One time when he was visiting
his house—as he'd long been a friend—
Eurytus blindly heaped abuse on him.
He claimed that, even though he had those arrows°
that could never miss the mark,
he was inferior to his own sons in proper archery.
He called him slave, cowed by a free man's word;
and then, when Heracles was drunk one night,
he had him thrown out from the house.
He was made furious by this,
and so, when Iphytus° arrived one day at Tiryns, 270
trying to track down his straying horses,
while he was distracted by his searching,
Heracles dispatched him off the platform of a tower.
It was because of this one deed
that mighty father Zeus was so incensed
that he exported him abroad for sale:
because this once he'd killed a man by trickery.°
If he'd retaliated openly,
Zeus would have pardoned him
because he would have justly thrown him down—
the gods detest such insolent behaviour as well. 280
And so Eurytus and his sons,
who'd been so overbearing with their words,
are all now lodged in Hades' house,
their town enslaved.
These women that you see in front of you
have had their lives degraded from prosperity.
And they have come to you,
as this is what your husband ordered,

and obedient to him I've done as told.
As for the man himself, as soon as he has made
his holy offerings to his father Zeus for victory,
you may be sure he will be here.
From this whole happy story,
that's the sweetest news for you to hear. 290

CHORUS-LEADER

So now, my lady, your full joy is clear to see,
some here before you, some the news of what's to come.

DEIANEIRA

I surely should be rightly glad on hearing
of this glorious exploit by my husband—
as of course my feelings should keep pace.
But, all the same, a person who thinks deep
about these things is bound to fear
that those who have success might one day trip.
This is because a piercing pity has, dear friends,
come over me from looking on these wretched women.
They have lost their homes and fathers 300
and are helpless in a foreign land.
Before this time they may have been
the daughters of free citizens,
but now they have a life of slavery.
O Zeus of battles, how I hope I'll never see
you turn against a child of mine like this.
[—or if you do, then not with me alive.°]
These fears of mine are stirred by seeing them.

She approaches Iole, the prisoner who is conspicuous.

Poor creature, who are you among these girls?
Unmarried? Or have you a child? (*no response*)
Your manner seems to say you're not experienced
in all these things°—and that you are of noble birth.
(*turns to Lichas*) Lichas, whose daughter is this stranger? 310
Who her mother, who the father that begot her?
Please tell me, since I pity her the most on seeing her,
as she alone knows what to feel.°

LICHAS
Why should I know? Why question me?
She may have been of quite high birth among them there.

DEIANEIRA
Might she be royal? Did Eurytus have a daughter?

LICHAS
Don't know. I didn't press too far with questions.

DEIANEIRA
Have you not learnt her name from her companions?

LICHAS
Far from it. I have done my job in silence.

DEIANEIRA (*to the woman*)
Tell me, poor woman, tell me for yourself. 320
I am unhappy at not knowing who you are. (*no response*)

LICHAS
It will be very different from the past if she does speak;
she hasn't said a single word,
but in the depths of grief has only kept on weeping
ever since she left the towers of her native town.
Her state is wretched, but we should be understanding.

DEIANEIRA
Let her alone, then; she can go in as she likes,
without yet more distress from me— 330
she has enough already.
Now let us all proceed indoors,
so you can hasten on to where you wish,
and I can manage things in there.

°*Lichas and the slave women go in; the old man intervenes to stop Deianeira from following.*

OLD MAN
Stay here a little, though, so you can learn,
without them here, just who these are
you're letting in your house; and find out matters

you should know, but have not heard.
Yes, I know all about these things.

DEIANEIRA

What's this? Why stop me when I'm on my way?

OLD MAN

Just stay and listen. What you heard from me before 340
was not a waste of time—it won't be now, I think.

DEIANEIRA

So should I fetch them back out here?
Or do you want to tell just me and these ones here?

OLD MAN

There is no need to be constrained
with you and them—just let the others be.

DEIANEIRA

They've all gone in. So tell us what you have to say.

OLD MAN

There's not one thing this man has just declared
that's strictly truthful: either he is lying now,
or else what he reported earlier was false.

DEIANEIRA

What? Say what you have in mind—
I have no notion what you're telling me. 350

OLD MAN

I heard this herald say in front of lots of witnesses
that it was all because of this young woman
Heracles destroyed Eurytus and his citadel Oechalia.
And Eros° was the only god who lured him to this war—
nothing to do with Lydians, or servitude to Omphale,
or Iphytus hurled down to death.
But now he's pushed Eros aside and tells another tale.
The truth is that, when he could not persuade her father
to give up the girl to be his secret mistress, 360
he devised a trivial pretext to invade her country,
claiming that Eurytus was a mere usurper there;
and so he killed her father° and destroyed her city.
And now, you see, he's coming, and has sent her

to this very house, not randomly,
not as a slave—no, don't imagine that:
that's hardly likely since he's molten with desire.°
That's why I thought it only right, my lady,
to reveal all this that I found out from him. 370
And lots of other people heard it too, the same as me,
there in the central meeting-place of the Trachinians;
so you can put this to the proof.
I'm sorry if what I report is far from nice,
but all the same this is the way it was.

DEIANEIRA

O god, what is my situation now?
What is this hidden torment
that I've let in underneath my roof, poor fool?
So she is nameless, is she, then,
as he who brought her swore?
—this girl so striking in her manner and her looks.

OLD MAN

She is the true-born daughter of Eurytus, 380
Iole by name.
That man could not tell you her birth—
because he hadn't asked indeed!

CHORUS-LEADER

Of all the wrong behaviour I deplore,
worst is the man who breaks his trust deceitfully.

DEIANEIRA

Women, what should I do?
I'm shattered by the things I've heard.

CHORUS-LEADER

Go ask the man himself. He might well tell the truth
if you can force him with strong questioning.

DEIANEIRA

Yes, I shall go. What you advise me makes good sense.

CHORUS-LEADER

Are we to wait out here? What should we do? 390

DEIANEIRA

Don't move; here comes the man out from the house,
and of his own accord, not fetched by me.

Lichas has entered as about to set off.

LICHAS

My lady, what am I to say to Heracles?
Instruct me since I am, as you can see, about to leave.

DEIANEIRA

How hastily you're on your way,
before there has been time
for us to go on with our conversation.

LICHAS

Well, if there's anything you want to ask, I'm at your service.

DEIANEIRA

And will you tell the whole and honest truth?

LICHAS

I shall, so far as I can know it—
may high Zeus confirm my words.

DEIANEIRA

Well then, who is that woman that you brought? 400

LICHAS

She is Euboean—who her parents were I cannot say.

°*The Old Man intervenes.*

OLD MAN

Hey, look this way: who d'you think you're speaking with?

LICHAS

And who are you to question me like this?

OLD MAN

If you have any sense, then answer what I ask.

LICHAS

To lady Deianeira, then, unless my eyes deceive me,
child of Oeneus, wife of Heracles,
and my own sovereign mistress.

OLD MAN
And that is why I wanted to make sure:
you say she is your sovereign?

LICHAS
And rightly so.

OLD MAN
Well, how should you be punished then, 410
if you are caught out wrongly treating her?

LICHAS
What wrongly? Why are you distorting things like this?

OLD MAN
I'm not. It's you who's doing that.

LICHAS
I'm off. I've been a fool to keep on paying you attention.

OLD MAN
No. Not before you've faced a simple question.

LICHAS
Go on then if you like. You are not one for keeping quiet!

OLD MAN
That prisoner, the woman that you took inside—
you surely know the one I mean?

LICHAS
I do. Why ask me this?

OLD MAN
Did you not say this woman that you brought—
don't look as though you do not know!—
was Iole, the daughter of Eurytus? 420

LICHAS
Said in what company? Can you find anyone
to witness that they heard the thing you claim?

OLD MAN

The citizens of Trachis, crowds of them,
were in the local meeting-place, and heard these things.

LICHAS

O yes, they may have said they heard,
but passing on impression's not exact reporting.

OLD MAN

What do you mean 'impression'?
Did you not declare on oath that you were bringing her
for Heracles to have as his bed-mate?

LICHAS

Me say 'to have as his bed-mate'?
Dear mistress, tell me who on earth this stranger is. 430

OLD MAN

One who was there and heard you saying
that her city was destroyed entirely by his wanting her;
that it was not the Lydian queen who brought it down in ruin,
but his passionate desire for her, this girl.

LICHAS

Please, mistress, tell this person to depart.
Someone of good sense should not
waste time disputing with a lunatic.

DEIANEIRA

Do not, by Zeus whose lightning strikes
the mountain glens of Oeta,
do not tell me false tales.
It's not some vicious woman that you're talking to,
nor one who's ignorant of how we humans are,
and how it's not our nature to stay constant
with the same delights for ever. 440
Whoever tries to pick a fight with Eros,
as if entering some boxing-match,
is acting like a fool.
For Eros lords it over even gods just as he likes—
and over me; and surely so another just like me.°
So if I were to hold my husband as to blame
for having caught this fever, I'd be mad.

And I can't blame this woman,
who's not responsible for something shameful,
nor for any malice aimed at me. Impossible.
So, if he has instructed you to lie,
then that is not an admirable lesson: 450
and if you've taught yourself like this,
then, though you might have hoped to be well spoken of,
you shall be looked upon as a disgrace.
So let me have the truth in full—
for a free man to be notorious as a liar
is a deadly mark of shame.
And it's impossible for you to get away with this,
since many that you spoke to will tell me the same.
And if you're acting out of fear for me, that fear is wrong,
because it's not the knowing that will give me pain.
What is so terrible in knowing?°
°Heracles has been to bed 460
with many, many women, hasn't he?
And yet not one of them has had to face
abuse or blame from me.
Nor shall this one, not even if he's utterly
consumed in his desire for her.
I felt a special pang of pity for her on first sight,
because her beauty has undone her life,
and has against her will
demolished and enslaved her fatherland.
Let all of that, though, sail off with the wind,
but you, I tell you this: while you may wrong another,
always tell the truth with me.

CHORUS-LEADER

Listen to this good advice. You'll never find 470
good cause to fault this lady; and you'll earn my thanks.

LICHAS

I see, dear mistress, that you think
in human terms, and not inflexibly;
and so I'll tell you all the truth without concealment.
Yes, it happened just as this man says:
a fearsome passion for this woman

thrilled through Heracles.
It was for her sake that her native city of Oechalia
was conquered and reduced to ruins.
And, to be just to him, he never told me
to conceal this, nor denied it: 480
that was all my fault, for fear of causing
your heart pain by telling the whole story—
if you regard that as a fault.
But now you do know everything,
I ask you for his sake, and for your own as well:
to be considerate towards this woman
by resolving to make good those words
you spoke concerning her.
You see, the man who has exerted supreme power
in everything has been completely conquered
by his passion for this girl.

DEIANEIRA

Well, that is what I mean to do, 490
and not inflict an added sickness on myself
by struggling against the gods.
Now let us go inside, so you can be entrusted
with the message that I send, and take the gifts
I should contribute in return for gifts.
It would be wrong for you to go back empty-handed,
when you've come with such a splendid retinue.°

They go inside, except for the old man, who slips away.

SECOND CHORAL SONG

CHORUS

Aphrodite has great might;
she always wins the prize.
I leave aside the tales of gods,
and how she took in Zeus, 500
and Hades and Poseidon too,
the god who shakes the ground.
But telling of this bridal-bed,°

which rivals took their stand?
Who entered in the ring
to win the marriage-prize,
landing blows with raining fists
and dust raised to the skies?

One was a mighty river-god,
a bull with threatening horns,
Achelous from Oini- 510
adai, four-legged in his form.
The other, armed with bending bow
and spears, from bacchic Thebes,°
shaking his great club, the son
of Zeus, great Heracles.
So they clashed together then,
both longing for her bed;
as umpire in between them came
sweet Cypris of the bed.

Then there was a battering
of fists and of arrows,
and there was a clattering
of horns struck in battle;
there were grips, and locking 520
limbs entwined in wrestling;
there was deadly crack of
heads, both of them straining.
While all through this the maiden
sat on a hill above them
looking down awaiting,
delicately lovely,
to see which one would bed her—
face all pale with panic,
trophy of the battle,
such a sight of pity.
Suddenly she's parted
from her mother's hold,
heifer separated
from her childhood herd. 530

SCENE 3

Deianeira comes back out by herself, carrying a metal casket.

DEIANEIRA

I've slipped out secretly to you, dear women,
while our visitor is talking to those
captive girls indoors before he goes.
I want to tell you of the action that I have in hand,
and seek your sympathy for what I'm going through.
I have, you see, let in a girl—
and yet no more a simple girl, I think,
a fully harnessed woman—
I've taken her on board,
the way a merchant stows a cargo;
but these goods will wreck my peace of mind.
And now the two of us shall lie
beneath a single coverlet, 540
and wait to see which one he will embrace.
Is this the kind of payment
that the so-called good and trusty Heracles
has sent me in return for caring for his house
through such a stretch of time?
I am not able to be angry with him
when he is afflicted with so virulent a fever,
yet what woman could bear living with her here,
and share in one man's making love?
I am aware how youth for one of us
is coming into bloom, and fading from the other;
and how men's eyes will turn from that
and want to pluck the flower.
And so my fear is that, while Heracles will be 550
in name my husband,
he shall really be the younger woman's male.
And yet, I say again, a woman of good sense
should not be ruled by anger;
so I'll tell you, friends, about the plan°
I have in mind to solve this situation.

°I have a present given to me long ago
by a primeval creature,
which I have kept secret in a flask of bronze.
I was still young when I first got it,
scooped up from the blood of Nessus as he died.
He was a shaggy-breasted Centaur,
and would ferry people for a price
across the swirling torrent of Euinos.
He used no boat with oars or sails, 560
but carried them himself. And so with me,
back when my father sent me on my way
as Heracles' new-bedded bride.
This Nessus hoisted me upon his shoulders.°
but once I was mid-stream,
he starts to touch me lustfully.
I screamed.
And Heracles turned round at once,
and sent a flighted arrow humming
deep into his chest.
Then with his dying breaths the creature said:
'Now, daughter of old Oineus, follow my advice
and then at least you'll get this benefit 570
out of my ferrying you—
because you were the last of all my passengers.
Collect the clots of blood from round my wound,
where they are blackened by the arrow-venom
cultured from the Lerna Hydra's fangs.°
This will then work for you as an enchantment
over Heracles to make quite sure
that he shall never love the sight
of any woman over you.'
I've thought of this, dear friends,
as ever since his death I've kept it
tightly shut away at home,
and have applied the substance 580
to this garment,° in the way he told me when alive.
And now that is completed.
I hope that I may never know or learn dark practices;
and I hate women who experiment with them:

but if I can in some way make this potion
work on Heracles with charms that will outbid
this girl, well then, the process has been set in place.
Unless you think I'm doing something crazed . . . ?
in that case I shall stop at once.

CHORUS-LEADER
As long as you are confident that this will work,
then we believe your plan is sound.

DEIANEIRA
I'm confident in my belief it will, 590
but I have never tested it in practice.

CHORUS-LEADER
Then you're about to do so,
since you can't be sure except by trying it.

DEIANEIRA (*noticing that Lichas is about to come out*)
We'll soon find out, as I can see him by the door,
and he will soon be on his way.
I only beg of you to keep my plan a secret.
If you try out something dubious, but keep it in the dark,
you'll never come down in disgrace.

Enter Lichas.

LICHAS
Please tell me, Deianeira, what I should be doing—
we're already lagging well behind our time.

DEIANEIRA
That is the very thing I have been seeing to, 600
while you were in there talking with those women:
here, this is a woven robe for you to take for me,
a gift for that great man prepared by my own hand.

She hands him the casket.

And when you give it to him, tell him clearly
that no one should put it on before he does;
and that no light of sun or altar-flame

or heat from hearth should shine on it—
until he stands conspicuous in view
and shows it to the gods upon a sacrificial day.
This is because I made a vow that, 610
if I ever saw or heard he'd come safe home,
then I would deck him in this robe
and so present him to the gods,
a brand new ministrant in new attire.
And you must take and show this seal upon these things,
one he will recognize, made by this signet ring.
Now go; and on the way respect the rule
that intermediaries should never interfere too much;
then you'll make sure of double gratitude
from him and me combined.

LICHAS
I'll faithfully perform the craft of Hermes, 620
and make no mistake in taking him this casket as it is,
along with your instructions.

DEIANEIRA
You may depart now that you have intelligence
of how things are within the house.

LICHAS
Yes, and I'll tell him how they've been secured.

DEIANEIRA
You know of that, because you saw yourself
the way the stranger-woman was received
and how I gave her friendly welcome.

LICHAS
I did; and I was pleasantly surprised.

Lichas begins to set off in the 'abroad' direction.

DEIANEIRA
What more is there for you to say? 630
I am afraid it is too soon to speak
of how I long for him, before I know
if I am longed for from that side.°

Deianeira goes inside.

THIRD CHORAL SONG

CHORUS

°All you who live about the thermal springs,
between the heights of Oeta and the anchorage
and gulf of Malis and the shore of Artemis,
site where the Greeks hold celebrated gatherings—
Thermopylae, the Gate of the Hot Springs—°

for you the pipes shall lift above their sound, 640
yes soon, fit for the gods in harmony,
to greet the son of Zeus and Alcmene,
as he is hastening homeward bound
and brings his prizes all triumphantly.

He's been distant from our land
while we've waited twelve long months;
far away across the sea,
us left in ignorance.
His devoted wife has wept, 650
worn away her heart in grief:
now, though, Ares frenzied° has
brought her pain-filled days relief.

May he come, yes, may he come;
may his vessel's many oars
make no stop until he lands
here upon this city's shores.
From Euboea° where we hear
he lights sacrificial fire,
let him come cloaked in the robe 660
which arouses his desire.°

SCENE 4

Deianeira comes back out in haste.

DEIANEIRA

I'm terrified, dear women, that I may have
gone too far in all that I did recently.

CHORUS-LEADER

What is it, lady Deianeira?

DEIANEIRA

I can't be sure, but I'm afraid it may emerge that
from my hoping for the best I've done great harm.

CHORUS-LEADER

You don't mean from your gift for Heracles?

DEIANEIRA

Yes, that. And now I would advise that hasty action
is mistaken when the aim is far from clear. 670

CHORUS-LEADER

Tell, if you can, what makes you feel such fear.

DEIANEIRA

A thing has happened that will strike you,
when I tell you, with astonishment.
I used a hank of white sheep's wool
for smearing on the robe, and . . . it's disappeared—
not cleared away by something in the house,
but more corroded from inside itself,
so that it's crumbled into nothing on the floor.
Let me explain more fully to you how it was.
I missed out none of the instructions 680
that the Centaur creature gave me
while the bitter barbs convulsed his frame,
but followed them as close as if they had
been carved indelibly upon a plaque of bronze.
These were his orders which I carried out:
I was to keep the potion always stored secure
away from fire and from the warming rays of sun,
until I should apply it fresh somewhere.
All that I'd done; and now the time had come,
I smeared it on in secret deep inside the house.
For this I used a hank of wool shorn from our flock; 690
and folded up the gift, and put it
well away from any gleam of sun

inside the lidded casket, as you saw.
Then, as I went back in, I saw a thing, unspeakable,
a sight beyond all human understanding.
I happened to have thrown that piece of wool down
where it lay in bright light from the sun.
[the sheep's wool used to smear there into flaming glare]°
As it grew warm, it lost its substance,
and disintegrated into crumbs upon the ground—
the thing it looked most like is saw-dust 700
that you see left where a man's been cutting wood.
As it lay there, the ground from underneath
came boiling up and spewed a kind of curdled foam,
most like the froth of grape-must, pressed out
from the purple fruit, when poured upon the ground.
I'm at a loss to know where I should turn my thoughts—
I realize I have done a fearful thing.
For why on earth should he . . . ?
What reason had the creature in the throes of death
to do me any kindness, when it was
because of me that he was dying?
It can only be that he bewitched me 710
so that he could kill the man who'd shot him dead.
And now, too late, when it's no use,
I come to realize this.
Unless my thoughts turn out quite false,
then I alone am going to prove the death of him.
I know the Hydra's venom on those arrow-barbs
caused even Cheiron° agony, although he was divine;
they mean sure death for any creature that they touch.
So this dark poison welling from that wound
is bound to kill this man as well—is that not so?
That's what I think; and so I have made up my mind
that, if he falls, then I shall die in that same swoop. 720
For any woman naturally noble
it would be unbearable to live on in disgrace.

CHORUS-LEADER

Such dreadful things are bound to stir up fears,
but don't despair before you know what's happened.

DEIANEIRA

For those who've made disastrous judgements
there's no hope that carries any confidence.

CHORUS-LEADER

When people make mistakes, but not deliberately,
then anger is less harsh—as it should be with you.

DEIANEIRA

Somebody not involved might say such things,
but not a person whose whole life is burdensome. 730

CHORUS-LEADER

Better not to go on saying more—unless you want
your son to hear, since here comes Hyllus,
who had set out earlier to find his father.

Enter Hyllus from 'abroad'.

SCENE 5

HYLLUS

O mother, how I wish for one of these:
that either you were dead;
or, if alive, you had been someone else's mother;
or somehow you could exchange your heart for better.

DEIANEIRA

What is it, son, that you so hate in me?

HYLLUS

Your husband, yes I mean my father,
you today, this very day, have killed him. 740

DEIANEIRA

Ah, what is this you tell me, child?

HYLLUS

A thing that's bound to come about,

since how can anyone make something
that's already clearly there not happen after all?

DEIANEIRA
What, child? Who gave you information
leading you to say I've done a thing so horrible?

HYLLUS
I've seen my father's gruesome fate with my own eyes—
not heard about it from another's talk.

DEIANEIRA
Where did you find and join with him?

HYLLUS
Well, if you have to know, I'll tell you everything.
When he had sacked Eurytus' famous citadel, 750
he'd brought his trophies and first-fruits of victory
and reached the sea-lashed headland
of Euboea called Cenaeum.°
He was there marking out a sanctuary and grove
devoted to his father Zeus; and that is where
I saw him first again, glad after missing him.
As he was just about to celebrate a splendid sacrifice,
his herald Lichas came from home
and brought your gift for him, the cloak of death.
He put this on, as you'd instructed him,
and then he sacrificed first-offerings,
a dozen flawless bulls, selected from 760
the hundred various animals he had assembled there.
At first, poor man, he offered prayers
with cheerful spirits, glorying in his splendid robe.
But as the blood-red flames flared
from the offerings and from the glowing oak,
a sweat broke out upon his skin,
and, tightly sticking, it began to cling
about his frame at every joint,
like drapery carved by a sculptor's hand.°
A gnawing pain began to wrack his bones, 770

and then a deadly poison, like the venom
from some snake, began to eat away at him.
At this he shouted out for Lichas
—though the wretch was no way guilty of your crime—
and asked what plot had made him bring this robe.
And he replied, in ignorance, it was a gift
from you and you alone, exactly as it had been sent.
As he heard this a piercing spasm
gripped his breast; he got a grip on Lichas
by the socket of his ankle joint,
and hurled him down to where he fell
upon a rock that stuck out from the sea.° 780
His skull was splintered and his creamy brains
all mixed with blood were spattered round.
The people there all cried aloud in horror
at the frenzied man and at his shattered victim.
No one dared to come near Heracles,
as he was twisting down and up with pain,
convulsing, shouting, screaming out;
and all the crags around resounded
from the hills of Locris° to the headlands of Euboea.
He hurled himself upon the ground repeatedly,
repeatedly cried out in agony, 790
and railed against the deadly marriage-bed
that he had joined with you,
the union made for him by Oeneus,
which had proved the ruination of his life.
And after this his frantic eye ranged
through the clinging sacrificial smoke and lit on me
as I stood weeping there among the crowd.
Then looking straight at me he called:
'Come near, my son; do not turn from my sorry state,
but, if needs must, then die along with me.
Now take me up away from here, and leave me
where no other human can set eyes on me. 800
Or, if you pity me, at least convey me from this place
quick as you can; don't let me die right here.'
We followed this command and set him in a boat,
and with great trouble rowed him,

groaning in his spasms, to this land.
And very soon you'll see him for yourself,
alive or just this moment dead.
These, mother, are the schemes and acts
against my father that you are convicted of.
For this may vengeful Justice and the Erinys°
now punish you.
If it is rightful, that's the curse I lay on you—
and it is right, since you have thrown away your right. 810
You've killed the greatest man of all upon the earth,
whose like we shall not see again.

°*Deianeira turns and goes indoors without a word.*

CHORUS-LEADER (*to Deianeira*)
Why turn away in silence? Don't you realize
your silence argues for the prosecutor's case?

HYLLUS
No, let her go.
I hope the wind may whisk her from my sight.
What point is there in holding high the name of mother
when her deeds are so unlike a mother's?
So away she goes—farewell to her!
I hope she may enjoy the same delights
as she has given to my father! 820

Hyllus departs indoors.

FOURTH CHORAL SONG

CHORUS
°You see this, girls, how suddenly
there has come to pass
fulfilment of the prophecy
from the distant past?
It claimed twelve years° of ploughshare-time
would have run their course
before the end of labours came
for the son of Zeus.
Time has steered that to its port

truly as it said:
for how could someone take on more
labours if they're dead? 830

°So if compulsion rakes at him
through the Centaur's tricks,
surrounding him with deadly mist
as the poison sticks—
the poison which Death brought about,
brewed with serpent's bite—
how could he possibly still see
another day's sunlight—
glued in the Hydra's fatal cloak
bristling with its goads,
and stirred by Nessus' deadly trick
through his seething words? 840

She, poor woman, felt no constraint,
since she foresaw great harm
from his newly-joined union
bearing down on her home.
Part she brought about herself;
part came through ideas she learnt
from that deadly encounter's lure.
Crying bitter lament
she must surely be shedding tears,
tender dew on her cheeks.
Fate approaching reveals deceit
as calamity breaks. 850

So the tears come pouring out
as his poisoning flows,
suffering more pitiable
than his enemies' blows.
Such disaster has been won
by his spear's bloodstained blade,
rushing from Oechalia
this newly-bedded bride
Cypris has been exposed behind 860
all these happenings here,

organizing them wordlessly—
now seen all too clear.

SCENE 6

A distressed cry is heard from inside.

CHORUS-LEADER
°Unless I'm wrong I heard just then
a sound of sorrow from inside the house.
(*another cry*)

CHORUS-MEMBER
What's this?
That cry was clearly one of anguished grief;
it means that something's happened there indoors.

The old serving woman comes out sorrowfully.

CHORUS-MEMBER
And look here, this old woman's coming out to us,
her face all sad and overcast. What can she tell? 870

OLD SERVING WOMAN
That gift, my girls, the one packed off to Heracles,
has been the start of mighty griefs.

CHORUS-LEADER
What new has happened then, old woman?

OLD SERVING WOMAN
Deianeira has embarked upon her final journey,
yet she has not moved a step.

CHORUS-LEADER
You can't mean she is dead?

OLD SERVING WOMAN
You've heard it all.

CHORUS-LEADER
She is already gone?

OLD SERVING WOMAN
You heard before.

CHORUS-LEADER
Poor woman! Say what way she died?

OLD SERVING WOMAN
By a most dreadful act.

CHORUS-LEADER
Tell us, old woman, how she met her end. 880

OLD SERVING WOMAN
A sword thrust to the heart.

CHORUS (*divided between members*)
What impulse, what affliction struck her dead?
How did she come to take that deadly blade?
How face the iron of that cruel sword?
How all alone was death on death contrived?
Did your eyes see the brutal way she died?

OLD SERVING WOMAN
Yes, I did see, as I was standing near.

CHORUS-LEADER
What happened? Tell us that. 890

OLD SERVING WOMAN
She made her own hand turn against herself.

CHORUS-LEADER
What are you saying?

OLD SERVING WOMAN
Simple truth.

CHORUS
Just born, just born within this house—
this newly-wed has spawned
a mighty curse.°

OLD SERVING WOMAN
Too true, too true. And if you had been there
and witnessed what she did, then your compassion
would be yet more deeply felt.

CHORUS-LEADER
And could a woman steel her hand to this?

OLD SERVING WOMAN

She could, and terribly.
I'll tell you to confirm my story.
When she had gone all by herself into the house, 900
she saw her son there in the courtyard
laying out a low-slung stretcher
so he could return and meet his father.
[then she shut herself away from sight°]
First she knelt before the altars
crying for the way that they would be deserted;
then went weeping as she put her hands
on all the household objects
that she used to use before.
She ranged this way and that throughout the house,
and when she met with some familiar servant,
she would weep in sorrow as she gazed at them,
lamenting both her own misfortune, 910
and the house bereft for evermore.
When she had done with that,
she rushed abruptly to the bedroom
that she used to share with Heracles—
I had a hidden view of this and watched it all.
I saw her spread the coverlets upon his bed;
when that was done, she got up onto it,
and settled sitting there.
As she wept streams of scalding tears,
she said, 'Farewell, my bed, my wedding-bed, 920
goodbye for evermore.
You never shall enfold me here again.'
And then with one firm movement,
she undid her dress from where the golden brooch
was pinning it above her breasts,
and bared the whole of her left shoulder and her side.
At this I ran with all the haste I could
to warn her son of her determination;
but within the time between my going and return,
she had, we saw, impaled her side 930
upon a sword and stabbed herself right to the heart.
Her son cried at this sight, because he'd come

to see how in his anger he had blamed her
for that crime; and now, too late, he'd learnt
from servants that unknowingly,
but worked on by the Centaur, she had done all this.
The poor boy then was struck with overwhelming grief,
and kept on weeping, planting kisses,
and he threw himself down side by side.
He bitterly lamented how he'd falsely 940
laid such damning blame on her,
and how he now would have to live bereft
of both of them, his father and her too.
So that is how things are; and anyone who counts
on two or more clear days ahead must be a fool,
because, until you're safely through today,
there can be no tomorrow.

The old serving woman goes back inside.

FIFTH CHORAL SONG

CHORUS

Which of these should I lament for first?
which of these disasters is the worse?
For me that is not easy to decide.
One is here in view within the house: 950
one is close, awaited in suspense.
To have and to expect are side by side.

If only a following wind
would carry me far from this land
before the immediate sight
of Heracles kills me with fright.
We hear he's returning again,
wracked with unbearable pain,
back to his dwelling-place here— 960
a vision too awful to bear.

A procession carrying Heracles on a stretcher, led by an old attendant, approaches slowly from the 'abroad' direction.

So they were not far off, but nearby,
when I shrilled the nightingale's cry—
look, here come some men from abroad.
Why bring him like this? With soft tread
they noiselessly carry him here,
like mourners for someone who's dear.
He's silent; how should we decide
if he's sleeping or if he is dead? 970

Hyllus comes out from the house just as the procession arrives.

SCENE 7

HYLLUS (*loudly*)
°O my father, such disaster!
What to suffer? What to offer?

OLD ATTENDANT (*quietly*)
Not so loud, son. Do not stir your
father's fierce and savage torment—
he's alive but is not conscious.
Bite your lip and keep your voice down.

HYLLUS
So, old man, he is still living?

OLD ATTENDANT
Don't disturb him from the sleep that
holds him; don't arouse the dreadful
fits of pain that leap upon him. 980

HYLLUS
But I'm overwhelmed with sorrow,
and my mind cannot restrain it.

HERACLES (*awakening*)
Zeus, what country have I come to?
Who are these around, me lying
wasted by relentless torment?
(*with cries of pain*)
Ah, again!
Ah, the guzzling pest devours me.

OLD ATTENDANT (*to Hyllus*)
Was I wrong to warn you it was
better to hold back in silence,
not to scatter sleep, and wake his
mind and eyes to full awareness? 990

HYLLUS
Yet I could not—I can't bear to
look upon this depth of torment.

HERACLES
O you altar, standing high on
Cape Cenaeum, such the thanks that
you have earned me in return for
all my sacrifices offered—
hear me, Zeus!
Such, such the damage
that you have inflicted on me.
How I wish I'd never seen you!
Then I never would have had to
face this lethal rash of madness.
Where's the chanter, where the 1000
skilful healer who could soothe down
this disaster—Zeus excepted?
Finding that would be a marvel!

The old attendant tries to make Heracles comfortable.

°Let me be, O let me be,
leave me sleeping wretchedly!
Stop that touching, turning me!
Deadly, you are killing me!
Such pain as had been calmed
you have re-inflamed.
It's got a grasp on me; it's creeping up again. 1010
Where have you gone, you most ungrateful Greeks?
I, who laboured ceaselessly to purge the wide world,
both sea-depths and forests! Yet now in the pit of my pain
is there nobody able to free me with fire or with iron?
(*with cries of pain*)

Won't someone strike my neck for me,
and finish hateful life for me?

OLD ATTENDANT

This task here has become too stubborn for my strength.
You, his son, should share this burden; you are born younger,
and can take more weight. 1020

HYLLUS

Here are my hands to help,
yet I possess no power to relieve his life or to obliterate
his agony, inside or out. It's Zeus assigns such things.

HERACLES (*recognizing Hyllus' voice*)

O my son, where are you, where?
Here, yes, here, lay hold of me;
lift me up, but lift with care.
It leaps, leaps, destroying me.
The menace, unapproachable,
preys on me, savage, cruel. 1030

Ah, ah, Athena,° here it is mangling me once more!
Feel pity for your father: draw out your sword, my son—
your blade will be blame-free—stab by my breast-bone here.
Heal this hellish pain maddened by your damned mother.
I long to see her fall just as she has laid me low

Sweet Hades, brother to Zeus, 1040
bring me sleep—end me, please—
with swift-swooping release.

CHORUS-LEADER

I shudder as I hear our master's sufferings—
for one so great to be tormented by such pain.

HERACLES

Many and perilous the labours I have undertaken
with my hands and carried on my back;
and yet not even Zeus' wife, nor loathed Eurystheus,°
have imposed on me a thing as cruel as this one
that the temptress child of Oeneus has enveloped 1050
round my shoulders, this fine-woven web
of the Erinyes, which is destroying me.

It has plastered fast around my ribs,
and has devoured my inmost flesh,
sucked out the channels of my breath;
it's gulped my living blood, and my whole body
is corroded by this overpowering cloak.
Not open battle, nor the earth-born forces
of the Giants,° not savage monsters,
nor anything in Greek or foreign lands, 1060
no country that I visited to purify—
none ever could do this.
And yet a woman, an unmanly female, she
has single-handedly defeated me without a sword.
(*turns to Hyllus*) My son, now show yourself to be my son in truth,
and do not rate the claim of 'mother' as superior.
With your own hands go fetch her here outside
and place her in my hands.
Then I can know for certain which you feel for more:
my tortured body, or else hers as it gets justly mangled.

Hyllus stays motionless.

Come, boy, endure it, 1070
pity me, most pitiable, reduced to weeping
like some girl—no one could say before
that they have seen me brought to this.
No—I used to bear all pains without complaint,
but now instead of that I am shown up as feminine.
Now come and stand beside your father here,
so you can see the kind of ways I'm suffering—
I'll show you how without concealment here.

He throws off his covering.

There, all of you, look on my wretched body,
witness what a pitiable state I'm in. 1080
(*cries of pain*)
This scorching pain is searing
through my frame again;
this ravening plague it seems
will never let me get outside its strangling grip.
Take me, lord Hades;
strike me, lightning from great Zeus;

hurl down your thunderbolt and shatter me.
Because it's eating me again,
it's breaking out, it's in full flood.
O hands, my hands,
and back and breast and trusty arms! 1090
°It was with these, with you, that I once overcame
with naked strength the settler in Nemea,
curse of shepherds, creature unapproachable
and unassailable, the Lion.
With you the Hydra-snakes at Lerna;
and the crew of isolated Centaurs,
double-natured with their horses' legs—
reckless, lawless, overbearing.
And you overcame the Erymanthian beast;
and that three-headed hound of Hades down below,
unbeatable monstrosity, the whelp of dread Echidna;
and the serpent that kept guard around
the golden apples at the furthest reaches of the world. 1100
I've taken on innumerable other quests,
and yet not one has triumphed over me,
and proved superior to my strength.
But now I'm devastated by this creeping plague,
disjointed, lacerated into shreds—
yes me, proclaimed the son of noblest mother,
and reputed as the child of starry Zeus.
Be sure of this, though: even if reduced to nothing,
even if immobile, I shall still close tight my grip
on her who has done this.
Just let her near me: then she shall be taught
to tell the world that still in death, as life, 1110
I've made the wicked suffer punishment.

CHORUS-LEADER

Unhappy Greece, what grief I can foresee
if you're to be bereft of this man here.

HYLLUS

Now that you let me offer some response,
please hear me, even in your sickness,
since I ask for what in justice should be granted.

Give me your attention, and do not allow
your pain to keep your anger still so biting;
otherwise you can not know how your resentment
and desiring for revenge is a mistake.

HERACLES

Say what you want and then be done. 1120
In my ill state I can't work out your subtleties.

HYLLUS

I'm going to tell you of my mother's case:
how she is now,
and how she did not purposely do wrong.

HERACLES

What? How dare you speak within my hearing
of the mother who has killed your father?

HYLLUS

Because it's wrong to keep unspoken how she fares.

HERACLES

Yes, very wrong to hide her evil-doings in the past.

HYLLUS

And you shall say the same about her deeds today.

HERACLES

Then tell me, but don't prove a treacherous son.

HYLLUS

I'll tell you straight: she's dead, just newly killed. 1130

HERACLES

Who killed her? This must be a sign, though sinister.

HYLLUS

She did it to herself—with no one else involved.

HERACLES

Damn her! Before I could kill her myself, as should have been.

HYLLUS

Even your fury would change course if you knew all.

HERACLES

So tell me what you mean by this strange start.

HYLLUS
She did a dreadful wrong, and yet she had meant well.

HERACLES
What kind of doing well is murdering your father?

HYLLUS
Mistakenly she thought she had a love-charm over you—
once she had seen the lover you'd brought home.

HERACLES
And who in Trachis could dispense a drug so strong? 1140

HYLLUS
Nessus the Centaur° long ago persuaded her
that she could send your passion frantic
with this potion's power.

HERACLES
O what a wretch I am!
I'm done, I'm dead, yes, dead,
I see the light of day no more.
Ah, now I understand the crisis where I stand.
My son, your father has no time to live,
so go and summon all your family by birth
together here, and summon poor Alcmene too—
who went to bed with Zeus to no avail!
Call them so they can hear the final oracle
I know about my death. 1150

HYLLUS
Your mother isn't here; she lives at Tiryns by the shore;
some of your children she has taken there,
while some are housed at Thebes within the town.°
But we are here for you, and shall obey
and do for you whatever you may ask.

HERACLES
Then listen what you have to do—
it's time for you to show what son of mine you are.
My father Zeus foretold me long ago
that I should never perish at the hand of one
who lives and breathes, 1160
but someone dead and lodged in Hades' house.

And so it is this Centaur creature who, as was foretold,
has killed me, living, though he's dead.
And I shall tell you of more recent prophecies
concurring close with these of long ago.
I visited the forest of the Selloi—
mountain priests who sleep upon the ground—
and I wrote down in full the message
sounded by my father's oak of many voices.°
This declared that at this very living time,
release would come from all the labours heaped on me. 1170
I thought this meant that I should go on happily,
but what it meant was I should die—
because no troubles are imposed upon the dead.
So since these things are clearly falling into place,°
you now must be my fellow-fighter;
do not wait until I'm forced to use fierce words,
but give assent and work along with me—
you'll find obedience to your father is the finest rule.

HYLLUS

Father, I am fearful now we've come to such a point,
but I shall still obey whatever you think right. 1180

HERACLES

First, then, with your right hand take hold of mine.

HYLLUS

But why put such a heavy pledge on me?

HERACLES

Give me your hand now, now! Don't disobey.

HYLLUS

Here, then, my hand. Your will is not to be denied.

HERACLES

Now swear this oath upon the head of Zeus, my father.

HYLLUS

Swear to do what? Is that to be disclosed?

HERACLES

Swear to carry through the deed that I prescribe.

HYLLUS
I take this oath, with Zeus my witness.

HERACLES
And pray for punishment if you don't keep to this.

HYLLUS
No need because I'll do it—all the same, I make the prayer. 1190

HERACLES
You know Mount Oeta,° sacred to almighty Zeus?

HYLLUS
I do. I've often stood up there for sacrificial rites.

HERACLES
You must lift up my body and convey it to that place
with your own hands, along with any friends you choose.
Next cut down ample branches from deep-rooted oaks,
and plenty from the male wild olive too;
then place my body on this wood,
and with a blazing torch of pine set it alight.
And let there be no weeping, but, as you are my true son,
do this with no lament, and with no tears. 1200
If you do not obey, I shall stay down below
a heavy curse upon you evermore.

HYLLUS
Ah, father, what is this you say?
What have you done to me?

HERACLES
I've said how you must act. If you do not,
turn into someone else's son, not known as mine.

HYLLUS
Ah no! You are demanding I become your murderer,
so that I have your blood upon my hands.

HERACLES
No, not at all, but the reliever of my present agony,
my one true healer.

HYLLUS
How can I heal your body, though, by setting fire to it? 1210

HERACLES

Well, if it's that you cannot face,° at least do all the rest.

HYLLUS

I'll not refuse the task of carrying you at least.

HERACLES

And heaping up the pyre as I've instructed you?

HYLLUS

Except that I shall not lay hand on it myself;
I shall do all the rest, and you'll have no complaint.

HERACLES

Well, that will do. And now add one
small favour to these greater ones.

HYLLUS

However great this thing, it shall be carried out.

HERACLES

You know the daughter of Eurytus, then?

HYLLUS

You're speaking, I suppose, of Iole? 1220

HERACLES

That's right. Now this is my command, my son.
This woman, once I'm dead:
if you desire to honour me and keep your oath,
make her your wife in bed.
Don't disobey your father;
don't let any other man but you possess her,
who has lain with me,
her body pressed to mine.°
Reserve this bed of marriage for yourself, my son.
Do it. Now you've obeyed me in great things,
to disobey in small would spoil the former favour.

HYLLUS

It must be wrong to feel enraged with someone sick, 1230
yet who could tolerate a sane man thinking such a thing?

HERACLES

It sounds as though you will do nothing that I ask.

HYLLUS

Who would . . . ? When she alone it is
who shares the blame for my dear mother's death—
and then for your condition too.
So who could choose this course—
unless demented by some demon of revenge?
No, father, I would rather die
than live with those I have most cause to hate.

HERACLES

So it appears this man will not respect my dying wish.
For sure the gods will keep a curse
for you if you do not obey. 1240

HYLLUS

I fear you're showing just how sick you are.

HERACLES

Yes, you have stirred awake my agony again.

HYLLUS

How these dilemmas crowd me in my misery!

HERACLES

Because you choose to disregard your father's wish.

HYLLUS

Then must I school myself to doing wrong?

HERACLES

Not wrong, when you would make me glad at heart.

HYLLUS

So you are fully justified in these commands?

HERACLES

I am—I call upon the gods as witness.

HYLLUS

I'll do it, then, and not resist,
displaying to the gods this deed as being yours. 1250
I never shall be blamed as wrong
as long as I'm obeying you, my father.

HERACLES

A good conclusion.

Add this favour too, my son, and quickly:
lay me on the pyre before some further fit
or tearing pain comes over me.
Now hurry, take me up.
This really is the last release from suffering,
and the final ending of this man, of me.

HYLLUS

There's nothing to delay these things from being done,
since you command them so compellingly, my father.

HERACLES

°Come then, move before you rouse this
sickness. Now, my stubborn spirit, 1260
fit a marble-clamping iron
bridle on my lips to stifle
cries of pain; so this reluctant
labour may conclude as welcome.

Heracles lies still on the bier.

HYLLUS

Come, my comrades, lift his body.
°Grant to me your deepest fellow-
feeling: but condemn the gods for
deepest lack of any feeling.
They get children and are famed as
fathers, yet look down indifferent
on such dreadful scenes of suffering.
No one can foresee the future, 1270
but this present shows us right for
pity, yet shows them as shameful.°
Worst must be the anguish of the
man who suffers this great torment.

CHORUS (?)

°You as well, young woman, do not
stay behind at home here, you who've
witnessed recent dreadful killings
and much new-inflicted suffering.
Nothing of all this is not Zeus.

°*All accompany the stretcher with Heracles off in the direction of the mountain.*

ELECTRA

INTRODUCTION TO *ELECTRA*

Electra's Emotional Turmoil

THE story of how Orestes returned from exile to avenge his father's death by killing his mother Clytemnestra and her paramour-become-husband Aegisthus was already celebrated in the *Odyssey* more than two hundred years before Sophocles. There is, however, no Electra there, and it is most likely that she was put on the mythical map by Aeschylus in the second play of his *Oresteia* trilogy of 458 BC.[1] This was regarded as his masterpiece and clearly continued to be very well known after his death. Electra is, however, secondary to Orestes in Aeschylus; she drops out of the play after the first half, and plays no direct part in the killings or their aftermath. Sophocles is very different. In Euripides' *Electra*, which we also have, she and Orestes are together most of the time, and have more or less equal roles:[2] in Sophocles she is by herself the central role.

Electra is, in fact, the only surviving Sophocles play which is dominated by a woman character throughout.[3] There are, of course, other powerful female roles—Iocasta, Antigone, Deianeira—but only Electra is on-stage and the centre of attention for almost the entire play. The prologue introduces her brother, Orestes, but he is then off-stage for a thousand lines, while Electra remains there throughout. On one level the play may be seen as a study in the shifting sequence of emotions and states of mind that she goes through as the story develops, a 'roller-coaster' of impulses and responses.

In the first two-fifths of the play (lines 86–660) she starts from unflagging grief and resentment, tinged with disappointment about Orestes, and then moves through disdain for her sister, then argumentative confrontation with her mother, mixed with disgust at her

[1] The Greek title of this play is *Choephoroi*, usually translated as *Libation-Bearers*; in my translation (published by Norton), I renamed it *Women at the Graveside*.

[2] There has been much debate among scholars over whether Euripides' *Electra* or Sophocles' came first—I am inclined to think it was the Euripides, but surprisingly little of serious significance for interpretation has been derived from any conclusion either way.

[3] There are several instances in Euripides, including Medea, Hecuba, and Helen.

sexual relationship with Aegisthus. In the next two-fifths (lines 661–1230) the news (false) of the death of Orestes produces immediate defiance out of her grief; and, provoked by her sister's resignation, she determines to face her own death in order to carry through revenge single-handed. Next, with the urn of Orestes' ashes (false) she reaches a new depth of grief. Her lament over the urn (1126–70) is generally regarded as the high spot, the most moving and memorable scene, of the play. Rather as the tragedy as a whole persuades the audience to experience the story as though it were real, so Electra—in a sort of 'play within a play'—persuades the audience temporarily that Orestes is dead, even though he is standing there.

In the last fifth of the play (lines 1230–1510) Electra is abruptly swept to the opposite extreme of overwhelming joy and jubilation. And in the final revenge sequence there is a complex overlapping sequence of emotions. She holds a grimly sardonic dialogue with her mother's death-cries, showing no trace of any softening or regret; then she plays cat-and-mouse with the hoodwinked Aegisthus. Finally she urges Orestes that he must not allow Aegisthus any chance to employ his argumentative talents (further on this dialogue see p. 134 below). Her last words show no softening or relaxation whatsoever (1487–90):

> No, kill him quick.
> And after killing him, consign him to the buriers
> who are right for him, well out of sight from us.[4]
> For me this is the only way for him
> to make amends for all his past of wrongs.

It is revealing to trace the way that these emotional responses are embodied in theatrical enactment through the use of stage space. In *Electra* it is far more than a mere convention that the action is set outside the doors of the background building—'this, the palace of the dynasty of Pelops, rich in blood', as it is described at the start (10). It is crucial to Electra's stand that she displays her defiance in public, discrediting the ruling regime, as she vigorously denounces her father's killers. She sees herself when she is indoors as a mere prisoner, a menial, while out in the light of day she can be a thorn in Aegisthus' side. It transpires that he even has plans to shut her away, princess

[4] This must mean the scavenging dogs and carrion birds—see note on 1487–8.

though she may be, in a subterranean cavern (378 ff.). Everything is changed, though, by the news of Orestes' death. Now she vows that she will never go into the house again, even if it means death (817–21):

> This I declare: I never more shall share
> a roof with them, not ever. I shall lie down friendless
> by this doorway here, and waste my life away.
> If any of those people there inside
> becomes incensed by this, then let them kill me.

When her sister Chrysothemis goes tamely indoors, Electra reiterates that she will never follow her in (1052). This theme of exclusion from the house gives extra power to her address to the urn, which she regards as the dead Orestes' home, almost as if Hades were inside it. She sent him away from the palace at Mycene, she laments, only to receive him back in the urn (1165–7):

> So now please let me in,
> receive me into this, your home,
> the nothing-me into your nothing-place,
> so I may dwell with you below for all of time.

Once the truth emerges, everything is changed, of course, and Electra does eventually go inside at line 1383 with full confidence. But this is only shortly before the final revenge, and soon she re-emerges with the task of looking out for the approach of Aegisthus. Once he arrives, she manipulates him until he is fully in the trap, and then urges Orestes to get on with killing him quickly—her last lines in the play (quoted above). She goes inside with the others at the end, but by then the future significance of the house has been put in question. Has it seen the last of the troubles of the dynasty of Pelops, or are there more to come? This question is inextricably tied up with the entire ethical interpretation of the play

Purifiers versus Contaminators

The rights and wrongs of Sophocles' *Electra*, and the responses to characters and situations which are indivisible from such ethical issues, have produced a fundamental split among critics. While there may be gradations and variations, there has been fundamentally a division between two 'schools', those who find that the play supports and endorses the justice of the claims of Orestes and Electra, and those who find that those claims are seriously flawed, or even condemned.

The former school might be called 'purifiers', and they maintain that this is a play of righteous revenge; that Clytemnestra and Aegisthus get what they deserve; and that the children will, as they and the chorus hope, resettle their heritage and live there happily ever after. For them the end of the play finally puts an end to the blood-stained and treacherous history of the royal dynasty.[5] The other school, the 'contaminators', find the claims of Orestes and Electra riddled with flaws, stained by warning signals that this is far from the end of the dynasty's troubles. They detect cracks in the arguments deployed by the pair in their defence; and they point to the recurrent allusions to the Erinyes ('Furies', see the note on lines 110–12), who in the Aeschylean version pursued Orestes after the matricide. But their case rests above all on the final scenes of the play, which will be discussed more fully below.

The whole tendency of critical, cultural, and political thought in the last thirty years and more has run against simple stances on matters of power and authority in favour of complication, subversion, and irony. This means that the purifying position has become increasingly less acceptable, and it would now be generally agreed to be untenably naïve. This still leaves the extent and degree of contamination open to discriminating gradation. Thus, although some contaminators find discoloration from the start, there is little during the first five hundred lines of the play that can be claimed to be clearly detrimental against Orestes or Electra. Her utterly uncompromising concentration on revenge for her father might be regarded as obsessive according to some modern values, but it is presented as loyally filial.

It is in the scene with her mother Clytemnestra (516–659) that cracks in Electra's casing of bravery and virtue begin to emerge.

[5] Purifiers tend to approve of the wording of lines 1505–7, the very last lines spoken by Orestes in our text:

> This punishment should fall upon all those
> who want to act outside the laws: yes, death.
> Then criminality would not be rife.

It is, however, pretty hard to defend them as authentic—see note on 1505–7.

Neither of them comes out well from their contest of arguments, and both have weaknesses exposed. Thus, Electra effectively attacks Clytemnestra's claim that her sole motive was to punish Agamemnon for his sacrifice of Iphigeneia by pointing to her conspiratorial adultery with Aegisthus. On the other hand Electra's defence of her father for the sacrifice is far from cogent. And when she warns her mother (lines 580–3) that the 'rule' of calling for death in payment for death will rebound on her, this must then apply to herself as well. And there is the recurrent motif of 'like mother, like daughter', which reflects on Electra as badly as it does on Clytemnestra. Electra herself does not deny the faults that she has learned from her (605–9):

> And so denounce me, if you like, to one and all
> as bad . . . or as foul-mouthed,
> or utterly without a sense of shame.
> Because, if I've been born with talents
> in exploits like these, then I do justice to the traits
> I have inherited from you.

The emergence of this element of inherited corruption had already been given some ominous preparation in the choral song immediately before the Clytemnestra scene. After a pair of stanzas that are implicitly in favour of Electra's stand, a final stanza at lines 503–15 suddenly and unexpectedly goes back three generations to Pelops, the founder of the dynasty that includes both Electra and Aegisthus (for more details see note on 503–15). Pelops had won his wife by deceitfully killing her father; and he had then repaid his agent, the charioteer Myrtilus, by killing him too. Since that time, the chorus sing (513–15):

> this house has never been safe
> free of calamitous strife.

So an idea is planted here. It is not, however, followed through in the central scenes of the play, and only re-surfaces towards the end. Again it is the chorus who raise the disquieting note. At lines 1397 ff. Electra is outside keeping guard while Clytemnestra is killed indoors. The mother's plea to Orestes for pity rings out, and Electra dismisses it with scorn, but the chorus' response in lines 1413–14 is ambivalent. Soon after, when Electra has urged Orestes 'Be strong: strike twice as hard!', the chorus have a snatch of more ominous lyric about how the dead are drinking the blood of their killers, which starts with the words 'The curses now begin their work . . .' (1416). The 'curses' are plural; this is not an end to them, but a continuation. This is only one hint of the underside, and from here on the whole situation becomes much darker. Once Aegisthus has fallen into the trap and realizes that he is facing his killer, Electra warns her brother not to let him talk—and her alarm is fully justified by what Aegisthus does manage to say in the last twenty lines.

When Orestes tells him to get inside, Aegisthus asks why, if this killing is such a good thing, it needs to be done 'in the dark'. Orestes' response that he wants to kill him where he had killed his father does not totally cancel out the allusion to darkness. And then Aegisthus comes out with a truly chilling question (1497–8):

> Is it inevitable that this house should witness
> all the horrors of the dynasty of Pelops,
> both those present and to come?

Not only does he recall that this is the house of Pelops 'rich in blood', but he stirs up the idea that its troubles are both present and future. Orestes does not—and perhaps cannot—challenge this threat of the future; instead he simply validates the present. When this invocation of what is yet to come intrudes so near the end of the play, the purifying interpretation surely becomes impossible to maintain without qualification. At the very least there is a shadow of contamination cast over the 'triumph' of Orestes and Electra.

Unfinished Business

While the extent and emphasis of the 'contamination' in the rest of the play is open to debate, what seems clear beyond reasonable question is that there is a cluster of disquieting factors during the final Aegisthus scene. And even more telling than the question about 'the horrors . . . to come' is the way that the play ends with Aegisthus still alive, not yet killed by Orestes. This 'unfinished death' is unique in surviving Greek tragedy, and it must have struck audiences as very strange. Elsewhere death scenes within the time-span of the narrative are always completed, and are nearly always followed by some kind of revelation or aftermath, often lamentation with or without justification or recrimination.

The most obvious comparison and contrast is with Aeschylus' *Oresteia*, where after the killings Orestes stands over the bodies and justifies his act, only to be pursued by the gathering Erinyes. There is then the whole third play of the trilogy which manages to reach some kind of resolution from the impasse. In Euripides' *Electra* both the killings are completed well before the end of the play. First, the body of Aegisthus is brought on and reviled by Electra; and then, after the killing of their mother, there is protracted remorse felt by the two children, so grim that not even Castor and Pollux, as 'gods from the machine', can impose a happy ending.

So what is the significance of the way that the death of Aegisthus is not completed before the ending of the play? It seems to me that the answer to this must be that the question of aftermath is also left unfinished, unanswered. Will Orestes and Electra succeed in occupying their ancestral heritage in peace? Or will there be future horrors for the dynasty of Pelops? Are there Erinyes waiting to pounce, as in Aeschylus? Will there be future unspecified trials and tribulations? Purifiers have tried to push the answers one way and contaminators the other. But what the play itself does is to postpone any answer. The future remains uncertain and the audience is left in suspense.

ELECTRA

LIST OF CHARACTERS

OLD SERVANT, Orestes' *paidagogos*, i.e. male carer from childhood

ORESTES, son of Agamemnon and Clytemnestra, who has been in exile since the murder of his father

PYLADES (silent), son of Strophius of Phocis, who sheltered Orestes in exile

ELECTRA, older sister of Orestes, who has stayed back in the ancestral home

CHRYSOTHEMIS, a sister of Electra and Orestes

CLYTEMNESTRA, formerly wife of Agamemnon and jointly responsible with Aegisthus for his death

AEGISTHUS, husband of Clytemnestra and ruler of Argos since the death of Agamemnon

CHORUS of women of Mycene

Place: in front of the royal palace at Mycene. One of the side-directions goes to the civic areas of the town: the other goes to the tomb of Agamemnon and then on abroad.

SCENE 1 (PROLOGUE)

Orestes, accompanied by Pylades, enters from the 'abroad' side, along with the old servant, who stands by him and points to the surrounding landscape.

OLD SERVANT

Now, son of Agamemnon,
[he who was commander of the host at Troy°]
°here you see before you all those sights
that you have been so eager to survey.
Here spreads the longed-for plain of ancient Argos,
sacred ground of Io, daughter of the river Inachus.
And that, Orestes, is the city gathering-place
beside Apollo's temple;
and to the left this is the famous shrine of Hera.
And here, this place we have arrived at,
is Mycene, rich in gold,
with this, the palace of the dynasty
of Pelops, rich in blood.° 10
From here I carried you away,
escaping from your father's murder;
and, instructed by your true-blood sister,
fetched you out and brought you up
to reach your present age,
and so avenge your father's death.
And now, Orestes, and you, Pylades,° his dearest friend,
you must decide, and quick, what should be done.
The glow of sunrise is already stirring up
the tuneful morning chorus of the birds,
and dark night's stars have left the sky.
And so, before there's anybody starting on their way 20
from out the house, you should discuss your plans.
Now's not the time for any more delay:
the moment's come for action.

ORESTES

Most cherished of all servants,°

see how clearly you display your loyalty.
Just as a thoroughbred, however old,
does not hold back in danger but pricks up his ears,
so you encourage us and stand out at the front.
So I shall tell you what I have decided,
and please give me your acute attention, 30
so that, if I miss the mark in anything,
you set me right.
When I approached the Delphic oracle
to ask what way I should best take revenge
upon my father's murderers,
Apollo answered me that I myself,
without armed soldiers in support,
should take my just revenge by using trickery.
So, following this oracle, your task is this:
to go inside this palace, when you get the opportunity,
and find out all they're doing there, 40
and then report to us with clear intelligence.
They will not recognize you after all this time,
and won't suspect you now that you've grown grey.
This is the sort of story you should tell:
that you're a visitor from Phocis,
come from Phanoteus,° who is their closest ally there.
And tell them, swearing it on oath,° about Orestes,
that he's dead, killed in a fall,
when he was hurtled from his racing chariot
as he competed in the Pythian Games.° 50
Make that your story.
Meanwhile, as told, we'll go and decorate
my father's tomb with offerings and locks of hair.
And then we'll make our way back here,
and bring that urn of beaten bronze
which we have hidden in the undergrowth.
That way we can deceive them with the welcome news
my body has gone up in smoke,
reduced to ashes in the funeral flames.
What is the harm, if playing dead in words
means I survive to carry off the glory? 60
No spoken word is bad, I think, as long as it brings gain.°

I've often heard the stories° told of clever men
reported falsely dead, who then returned
back home to even greater honour.
Just so, I claim that from this lie
I'll come to shine star-like above my enemies.
(*praying*) So now, land of my fathers, and you local gods,
grant me a welcome and good fortune in this quest.
And you as well, ancestral home,
because, encouraged by the gods,
with justice I advance to purge you clean. 70
Don't send me from this land without my rights,
but make me master of my wealth and heritage,
re-founder of this house.
That's what I have to say.
And now, old man, you go and take care of the things
that are your task, and we two shall set off.
The time has come, and seizing the right moment
is the most important key
to every human enterprise.

ELECTRA (*heard from indoors*)
O, what a wretched thing I am!

OLD SERVANT
I thought I heard some servant here indoors
complaining in distress, my son.

ORESTES
Poor woman, might it be Electra? 80
Do you think that we should stay
and hear what she laments?

OLD SERVANT
No, definitely not. Try nothing else
before we've made a start by doing what Apollo said,
So first pour out libations for your father—
that is what will bring us victory
and control of what is done.

They go off as Electra comes out from the palace.

SCENE 2

ELECTRA

°Limpid sunlight and you upper
sky that share in dawn,° how often
have you heard my songs of grief, how
often have you seen me score my
breast to lacerated bleeding 90
when the dark of night is over.
And my hateful bed inside this
dismal dwelling knows full well my
night-long weeping, as I grieve for
my humiliated father.
Ares war-god did not grant him
honours in a foreign country:
no, my mother and her mate in
bed, Aegisthus, swung a deadly
axe and cracked his skull the way wood-
cutters split apart an oak.
Mourning cries, dear father, come from 100
no one else but me, although your
death was pitifully dreadful.
Even so I'll never stop my
bitter dirge of lamentation,
not as long as I can see the
stars all sparkling and this daylight.
No: before this doorway of my
father's palace, I shall, like the
nightingale° who killed her offspring,
raise my cry so all can hear it.
O you house of Hades and Per- 110
sephone, and chthonic Hermes,
and you, potent Curse, and awesome
goddesses Erinyes,° you
who can see those foully murdered,
and adulterers in secret:
gather, help me, give me vengeance,
payment for my father's slaughter.

And I beg you, send my brother,
since I have the strength no longer
to outweigh this overbearing
load of anguish by myself. 120

The chorus come on from the city side.

FIRST CHORAL SONG (PARODOS)

(*in lyric dialogue with Electra*)

CHORUS

°Daughter, Electra, daughter
born of worst of mothers,
why waste away for ever,
insatiably mourning
for the obscene, treacherous
death of Agamemnon,
victim of vicious plotting
by that scheming mother?
I curse the perpetrator,
if such a prayer is proper.

ELECTRA

Noble friends, you've come here
offering me comfort 130
in my pain, I know that,
I'll not surrender,
nor desist from grieving
for my wretched father.
You who show me friendship
with all kinds of favour,
leave me to my raving—
let me be, I beg you.

CHORUS

All the same you can never
resurrect your father
from the deep marsh of Hades,
pit for every human,

no matter how much grieving.
All this pointless wailing
going beyond all reason 140
becomes self-destroying,
and no relief from trouble.
Why desire such turmoil?

ELECTRA

It's a stupid person
who could rest unmindful
of a parent's dreadful
ending. There is one who
fits my state: the bird who
mourns for Itys, Itys.°
And you, all-enduring
Niobe,° for me god- 150
like, in your rock-formed
tomb you weep for ever.

CHORUS

You are not the only human
who has sorrow given,
but your grief has been excessive—
some are less intrusive:
like Chrysothemis, they're living
sisters quiet within.°
Also think about that other,
young and safe from trouble;
with good fortune one day he'll be 160
welcomed to Mycene,
coming here, as Zeus blesses—
nobly born Orestes.°

ELECTRA

And I wait for him unending,
with no children and no wedding,
as I drift here drenched with weeping,
and oppressed by grief unceasing,
while he seems to be forgetful
of the suffering he should know well.

All the messages he sends me 170
merely seem to be deceptive—
always saying he is longing:
even so for all this longing,
he always seems to have some reason
never to appear in person.

CHORUS

Courage, take courage, daughter:
Zeus is still almighty,
from heaven ruling over
all things in his power.
Entrust to him your anger;
don't hate too much. Remember
the son of Agamemnon
lives yet in Crisa's meadow,° 180
and keeps keen awareness—
as does the great god Hades.

ELECTRA

As for me, my life's gone passing,
leaving me with all hope missing,
lacking strength, becoming dwindled,
never able to have children,
with no husband as my champion.
I am like a stateless chattel,
working as a servant, helpless
in my own ancestral palace, 190
clothed in these degrading tatters,
hanging about empty tables.

CHORUS

°Pitiful scream when he came home,
pitiful feast in his own home,
when on that day the axe's blade
brought down its edge upon his head.
Trickery the means that laid the plan,
lechery the urge that killed the man.
They begot a deadly dreadful scene,
whether god or mortal had this done. 200

ELECTRA

O far the most hateful light
that's dawned in my whole life!
O night, the anguish that pierced
at that most monstrous feast!
My father there faced his death,
handiwork of them both—
hands that have left me betrayed,
have left my life destroyed.
May Zeus ensure they are paid
in pain returned for pain, 210
and never enjoy that wealth,
fruit of the deed they dealt.

CHORUS

Take my advice, do not say more:
you see who holds the present power.
Why plunge yourself so recklessly
so deep in self-destructive misery?
You've made troubles that are too harsh
as you breed battles for your own heart.
There's no point wrestling those in power,
so bear these sufferings as they are. 220

ELECTRA

I know this well: my rage
is terror pushed to the edge.
Yet in bad times should I keep grief
restrained? Not while I live.
Who, friends, with mind that is clear
could think that I could hear
words soothing sorrow away?
Let go advice, let go.
Anguished beyond relief
I'll never drop my grief. 230

CHORUS-LEADER

Well, I say this meaning kindly,
like a trusted mother, do not
breed disaster on disaster.

ELECTRA

What could be a good amount of bad?
Can it be right to disregard the dead?
Could that thrive in any human heart?
I never want respect from such as those, 240
joining them to live a life of ease.
I'll never clip the wings of shrill lament,
not by holding father in contempt.
If he's to lie, a nothing, in the earth,
cold, while they don't pay for death with death,
why, then Respect would leave the world behind;
Decency desert our humankind. 250

SCENE 3

CHORUS-LEADER

We've come, dear child, to bring you our support,
and for ourselves as well. But if our words strike you
as wrong, then you prevail, for we shall go along with you.

ELECTRA

I am embarrassed, women: I must seem to you
so overwhelmed with all my lamentation;
yet I'm driven to behave this way,
so please be understanding.
How could a noble woman not respond like this
when she confronts her father's degradations?
And day after day I see them growing, never less. 260
First, my relations with the mother who begot me
have descended to the depths of loathing.
Next, I have to go on living in the house
shared with my father's murderers;
they have control of me, and they dictate
what I can have and what to go without.
And then imagine how I spend my days,
when I have got to watch Aegisthus
take his seat upon my father's throne;

and see him strutting in the robes
he used to wear, and pouring out libations
by the very hearth he killed him at. 270
°And see the crowning act of their contempt,
I mean the killer lolling in my father's bed
beside my sordid mother—
if the name of mother's proper for the woman
who indulges copulation with this man.
She has the gall to live with that polluting filth,
yet feel no fear of any vengeful spirit.
°On the contrary, as though exulting in her deeds,
she keeps the day on which she killed my father by deceit,
and organizes choruses each month 280
and sacrificial offerings to her guardian gods.
I have to see all this inside the house:
and there I weep, I waste away,
and have to hold inside myself my cries against
that feast which grossly bears my father's name,
kept to myself since I'm not free to grieve enough
to bring my heart relief.
And she, that noble woman,
shouts and hurls complaints like these:
'You god-forsaken girl,
are you the only person who has lost a father?
Is there no one mourns except for you? 290
To hell with you! I hope the gods below may never
give you respite from the grief that grips you now.'
That's how she rants at me—except for when
she hears some talk about Orestes coming back;
and then she stands and screams with fury in my face:
'You are the one to blame for this, aren't you!
It was your doing when you stole Orestes
from my grasp and got him secretly away.
You'll pay for this, make no mistake!'
She yaps that kind of thing,
and all the while her celebrated bridegroom 300
tags along and eggs her on—
this utter weakling, yes, this total blight,
this man who only fights with help from women.

And meanwhile I'm exhausted,
waiting here for ever for Orestes to arrive
and put an end to this.
By constantly delaying on the point of action
he's destroyed my hopes, both real and unreal.
In such circumstances, friends, it is impossible
to be restrained or show respect.
But in bad times bad ways become necessity.

CHORUS-LEADER

Aegisthus—is he nearby while you're saying 310
all these things? Or is he gone away from home?

ELECTRA

Most certainly away. You don't imagine
I would venture out of doors if he were here?
He's in the countryside for now.

CHORUS-LEADER

If that is so, I might more confidently
share in conversation with you.

ELECTRA

He is not here, so go on, ask me what you want.

CHORUS-LEADER

I wonder what you're thinking of your brother:
is he coming—or delaying? I would like to know.

ELECTRA

He claims he's coming, but he doesn't turn this into deeds.

CHORUS-LEADER

Yes, men are liable to hesitate before a weighty act. 320

ELECTRA

Well, I'd no hesitation when I rescued him.

CHORUS-LEADER

Don't fret. He's noble, and he'll help those dear to him.

ELECTRA

So I believe, or I would not have stayed alive this long.

SCENE 4

Chrysothemis emerges from the door, carrying offerings.

CHORUS-LEADER

Now don't say more, because I see your sister
coming out of doors, Chrysothemis,
—same father as you, and same mother too.
She's carrying the kind of offerings
customary for the dead.

CHRYSOTHEMIS (*abruptly to Electra*)

What is it you have come out to proclaim
before the entrance doorway, sister?
Have you not learnt the lesson after all this time 330
not to go indulging in your pointless rage?
And yet I know this for myself:
I do not like the way things are,
and so much so that, if I only had the strength,
I'd show them clearly what I think of them.
But I've decided that it's best to shorten sails
in stormy times, and not appear aggressive
when there is no chance of harming them.
I only wish that you would do the same.
Although I know the right lies not with what I say
but with your judgement, still, if I'm to lead
my life at liberty, that means complete compliance
with the will of those in power. 340

ELECTRA

It's terrible that you neglect the father
you were born from, and devote
your loyalty to your mother's side—
all this reproaching me is learnt from her,
and none of it comes from yourself.
So make your choice: to give up being sensible,
or, by being sensible, abandon those you should hold dear.
You said yourself just now that if you had the strength
you would reveal how much you hate them;
yet, when I do all I can to get our father his revenge,

you will not work with me,
and put me off from doing anything. 350
Does this not simply add on cowardice to being wrong?
For tell me—or let me tell you—what benefit
would come from giving up on my complaints?
I am alive, aren't I?
—wretchedly, I know, but still enough for me.
What's more, I cause them hurt, and that way give the dead
due honour, if some gratitude is felt down there.
Your hatred is no more than hate in words:
in fact you go along beside your father's killers.
I . . . well I would never, not if loaded with the goods 360
you revel in, I never would give in to them.
You can have your fancy fare and life of luxury,
but grieving will be sustenance enough for me.
I've no desire to share your kind of privilege—
nor would you if you had sound sense.
So while you could have had renown as daughter
of the best of fathers, you get called instead
your mother's girl. That is the way to be the most despised,
through your betrayal of our father and your own.

CHORUS-LEADER

Don't speak in anger, please—
there's merit in what both of you have said, 370
if you would learn her lesson and she yours.

CHRYSOTHEMIS

I have some knowledge, women, of her kind of talk.
I'd not have raised this issue, were it not
that I have heard of deadly trouble looming up for her,
enough to stop her from her long-drawn-out laments.

ELECTRA

Well then, what is this dreadful threat?
If you can tell me something worse than what I have,
I'll not continue contradicting you.

CHRYSOTHEMIS

All right, I'll tell you everything I know.
They're going—if you don't stop this complaining—
they are going to put you somewhere 380

where you'll never see the sun:
instead you'll be shut living in an excavated cell,°
outside this land, where you can go on singing hymns of woe.
So give that thought, or later when you're suffering,
do not lay blame on me.
Now is the time to show some sense.

ELECTRA
Is this how they've decided what to do with me?

CHRYSOTHEMIS
It is, the minute that Aegisthus gets back home.

ELECTRA
The quicker that he comes the better then.

CHRYSOTHEMIS
What's this you're calling down upon yourself?

ELECTRA
That if he means to do these things, then let him come.

CHRYSOTHEMIS
So that you suffer what? What are you thinking of? 390

ELECTRA
So I can get as far away as possible from all of you.

CHRYSOTHEMIS
But don't you care about the life you have?

ELECTRA
Oh yes! This life of mine is wonderful!

CHRYSOTHEMIS
It might be if you could just learn some sense.

ELECTRA
Don't teach me to betray the ones I hold most dear.

CHRYSOTHEMIS
I'm not—but to submit to those in power.

ELECTRA
You can play sweet with them:
that's not the way that I behave.

CHRYSOTHEMIS
Yet it's no good to fall through being foolish.

ELECTRA
I'll fall if need be in a father's cause.

CHRYSOTHEMIS
I'm sure our father is forgiving in this case. 400

ELECTRA
It's typical of cowards to lean on words like that.

CHRYSOTHEMIS
Well, be persuaded and agree with me.

ELECTRA
No, no, I never want to be so empty of all sense.

CHRYSOTHEMIS
In that case I shall set about my errand.

ELECTRA
Where are you going to? Who are these offerings for?

CHRYSOTHEMIS
Our mother says to pour them on our father's tomb.

ELECTRA
What? Offerings for her deadliest enemy?

CHRYSOTHEMIS
The one she killed herself—as you so like to say.

ELECTRA
What friend persuaded her? Or whose idea was this?

CHRYSOTHEMIS
I heard she had some nightmare dream. 410

ELECTRA
Ancestral gods, be with me now at least!

CHRYSOTHEMIS
Are you emboldened by this fear of hers?

ELECTRA
If you can tell me what she dreamt, then I could say.

CHRYSOTHEMIS
I only know a little bit of what she saw.

ELECTRA
Well, tell me that at least. A little tale has often
brought down human fortunes or has set them up.

CHRYSOTHEMIS

It's said that in her dream she went a second time
together with our father,° yours and mine,
come back to life. And then he took the sceptre,
which he used to hold, and now Aegisthus has,
and planted it beside the hearth. 420
From that there grew a trunk that sprouted leaves
and cast its shade across the country of Mycene.
This is what I heard from someone who was there
when she revealed her vision to the Sun outside.
I know no more except that it's because
she is afraid of this that she has sent me out.
[And so I beg you by the family gods to follow my advice
and not to come to grief through foolishness.
If you reject me then you will come back to me in trouble.°] (430)

ELECTRA

Dear sister, don't place any of these things
you're carrying upon the tomb—
it is not right or holy to bring offerings
to our father from his hateful wife.
No, throw them to the winds,
or hide them buried underneath the earth
where none of them can ever reach
our father's resting-place.
Let them instead remain preserved below
as treasures stored for her when she shall die.
If she were not the hardest-hearted woman ever born,
she never would have sent these rancorous libations 440
to the graveside of the man she killed.
D'you think the dead man in his tomb would gladly take
these offerings from the one who cruelly killed him—
at whose hands he had been mutilated
like some foreign enemy; the one who tried
to clean away pollution by then wiping off
his blood on his own hair?°
D'you really think these things could
purge her of the murder-guilt?
Impossible. So throw these offerings away:

instead cut off a lock from your own hair,
and one from me as well—it's slight but all I have; 450
and offer these to him, this unkempt lock
and this plain waist-band with no ornament.

She hands the lock of hair and belt to Chrysothemis.

And after you have fallen down and prayed to him
to come with favour from beneath the earth
and give us help against our enemies,
then pray in hope about his son Orestes:
that he stays alive to get the upper hand,
and plant his foot upon his enemies;
and then in future we may decorate his tomb
more richly than with what we can give now.
For I believe—I do believe—that he too had a part
in sending this unwelcome dream to her. 460
Yet do this ritual, sister, and so reinforce
yourself and me, as well as him most dear,
our father, laid below.

CHORUS-LEADER

What she suggests is pious; and, dear girl,
if you have proper sense, you'll do this thing.

CHRYSOTHEMIS

And so I shall; for what is just should not
be argued with and calls for urgent deeds.
But as I try to put these in effect,
I beg of you, dear friends, keep quiet,
since if my mother should find out, 470
I fear this enterprise would turn out bitterly for me.

Exit Chrysothemis towards the tomb; Electra remains.

SECOND CHORAL SONG

If I'm not an erring prophet,
lacking insight in my mind,
Justice is, as foretold, coming,
bearing just power in her hand,
coming not far in the future.
Boldness newly fills my heart,

now I've heard about this vision, 480
welcome wafting through the night.
For your father, great Greek leader,
shan't forget, though cruelly laid
low, nor shall the ancient deadly
axe of bronze with double blade.

With many feet and hands she's coming,
flitting from her ambush place, 490
bronze-clawed Erinys,° to catch them
eager for their lewd embrace,
forging an unbed, unmarriage.°
I'm emboldened by this dream,
which shall never grant acquittal
for the partners in this crime.
Oracles and dreams mean nothing 500
for us mortals here on earth,
if this nightmare and its terrors
do not sail through to their berth.

°Calamitous was that horse-race,
which Pelops won through a cheat;
it's taken its toll on this place.
For, since Myrtilos drowned in sleep
enclosed in the ocean's lap,
hurled down from the golden step 510
of his chariot by foul deceit,
this house has never been safe
free of calamitous grief.

SCENE 5

Clytemnestra appears abruptly in the doorway.

CLYTEMNESTRA

So here you are, out on the loose again.
That is because Aegisthus isn't here;
he's always kept you in to make quite sure

you don't disgrace the family—
at least not out of doors.
But now that he's away, of me you take no notice,
even though you've often publicly declared 520
that I exert my power beyond what's right,
dismissing you and yours with mere contempt.
But I am not contemptuous;
I only say unpleasant things of you
because you often do the same to me.
You always cite your father, that one cause,
as your excuse, alleging that he died through me.
Well yes, I know it was 'through me'—
I cannot possibly say no to that,
as Justice, and not I alone, put him to death.
And you should add support if you had sense,
because this father you're for ever moaning for, 530
°he was the one, and he alone, who steeled himself
to sacrifice your sister to the gods—
though when conceiving her it was not pain he felt°,
no pain to match mine giving birth!
And next just tell me this: who did he sacrifice her for?
Do you reply 'the Greeks'?
They had no right to sacrifice my child.
Or for his brother Menelaus?
Then shouldn't he have paid the price instead—
has he not got a pair of children of his own?
They should have died, not her, since this whole venture 540
was to serve their father and their mother's cause.
Or else had Hades got some urge to feast upon
my children more than hers?
Or did your cursèd father lack the pull of love
towards the children borne by me,
yet felt it for his brother's?
Would that not be a twisted way of thinking for a father?
That's what the poor dead girl would say if she could speak.
So I feel no disquiet for what was done to him.
And if you think that I am in the wrong, 550
then find good judgement for yourself
before you criticize those next to you.

ELECTRA

For once you cannot claim that I began
with some unpleasantness before
I had to hear all this from you!
But, if you will allow, I'd like to set things straight,
both for the dead man and my sister too,

CLYTEMNESTRA

I do permit it. If you would always speak like this,
it wouldn't be distasteful hearing you.

ELECTRA

Then I shall speak.
First. you confess you killed my father.
There's no admission could deserve more shame,
no matter whether just or not. And it was not 560
with justice that you killed him; you were dragged astray
by prompting from a vicious man—the one you're living with.
°And then ask Artemis what was she punishing
when she held back the winds at Aulis?
Or since it is not right to question her, I'll tell you.
My father, so I've heard, was hunting game
within her sacred grove, and, as he trod,
he started up a dappled stag; and, when he'd brought it down,
he let slip out a boastful phrase about the kill.
Enraged by this the goddess stopped the Greeks; 570
and so my father had to sacrifice his daughter's life
as compensation for the animal.
That is the explanation for her sacrifice:
°there was no other way to get the army free,
neither back to home nor on to Troy.
This way he was obliged and forced to sacrifice her,
much against his will—not for the sake of Menelaus.
But even had he done this for his brother's sake,
to put your case, how was it right for him
to meet death at your hands for this?
According to what rule? Beware in case,
by making this a rule for humans, 580
you regret the hazard you are posing for yourself.
For if we're meant to claim a death for death,

then you should be first to die and get your just deserts.
But now I'll make you see how the excuse you claim is empty.
Tell me, please, how does it come about
that you are now committing acts
that dredge the depths of shame?
You're sleeping with that poison filth,
the man who previously helped you kill my father.
And you're getting children with him,
casting out your previous offspring,
even though they're good and from good stock. 590
How could I give approval to that choice?
Or are you going to claim that this as well
is retribution for your daughter?
That would be a sordid claim:
it can't be right to have sex with your enemy,
and say it's for your daughter's sake.
But no, I'm not allowed to give you good advice,
as you full-throatedly proclaim
that I bad-mouth my mother. And it's true
that I consider you a tyrant rather than a mother,
as I live out my wretched life surrounded
with the many disadvantages I get
from you and your conspirator. 600
As for that other one abroad,
who only just escaped your clutches,
poor Orestes: he grinds through a wretched life.
You have accused me often that I've brought him up
to punish you—and yes, if I had only had the power,
you may be sure I would have done.
And so denounce me, if you like, to one and all
as bad because of that, or as foul-mouthed,
or utterly without a sense of shame.
Because, if I've been born with talents
in exploits like these, then I do justice to the traits
I have inherited from you.

CHORUS-LEADER

°I see you fuming at her words, 610
not caring any more if she has justice on her side.

CLYTEMNESTRA

How should I give a damn for her
when she has treated me with such contempt?—
and her so young! She'd surely go
to any lengths without a scrap of shame!

ELECTRA

But I do feel ashamed, you know,
despite whatever you may think;
I know I'm acting wrongly for my age, improperly.
But your ill-will and what you do compel me
to behave like this despite myself—for bad behaviour 620
gets instructed through bad deeds.

CLYTEMNESTRA

You shameless creature, all my words and acts achieve
is to provoke you to speak out too much.

ELECTRA

It's you who talk not me, because it's you who acts;
and it is actions that find out the words.

CLYTEMNESTRA

I swear by lady Artemis: you shall pay dear
for all this insolence once that Aegisthus comes.

ELECTRA

You see? You're in a fit of fury, even though
you gave me leave to say the things I wanted.
You're incapable of listening.

CLYTEMNESTRA

Just stop ill-omened shouting, and allow me peace 630
to sacrifice, now I've allowed you all your say.

ELECTRA

Go on then with your sacrifice;
don't hold my voice to blame, as I shall speak no more.

CLYTEMNESTRA (*standing before the statue of Apollo and addressing her maids*)

Attendants, hold up high these fruitful crops,
my offerings to lord Apollo here, along with prayers
to free me from the fears that grip me now.
°Please listen, guardian Phoebus, to my hidden meaning,

hidden since I am not speaking among friends,
which makes it inappropriate for me to disclose everything—
not while this one is standing close, 640
who, as I know of her resentment and her ranting tongue,
would scatter ugly rumours through the town.
So listen in that light, because I have to cover it like this.
The dream I've had this night just past
might be interpreted in two opposing ways.
If it is favourable, then grant it be fulfilled:
but if it's dangerous, then turn it back upon our enemies.
If there are those who are conspiring secretly
to cast me out from my prosperity—
do not allow them.
No, but let me always live like this,
a harm-free life, controlling these ancestral powers, 650
and living with those dear, the ones I live with now,
enjoying happy times with them
and with those children who do not
maliciously wish bitter pain for me.
O lord Apollo, listen favourably to this,
and grant me everything just as I ask.
As for the rest, I think that even with me keeping quiet,
still you, a god, must understand it well.
[for Zeus' children must be able to see everything°]

The old slave, pretending to be a messenger, enters from the 'abroad' side, while Clytemnestra is turned away towards Apollo.

SCENE 6

OLD SERVANT
Please tell me, women, can I know for sure 660
this is the palace of Aegisthus, ruler here?

CHORUS-LEADER
It is indeed—you have supposed that rightly.

OLD SERVANT
And would I rightly guess this lady is his wife?
She looks like royalty.

CHORUS-LEADER

You are completely right—and here she comes to you.

Clytemnestra turns and approaches.

OLD SERVANT

My greetings, lady. I am bringing pleasing news
for you and for Aegisthus from a friend.

CLYTEMNESTRA

I welcome the good omen.°
First of all, then, tell me who has sent you here.

OLD SERVANT

Lord Phanoteus of Phocis—and the message is important. 670

CLYTEMNESTRA

What is it, stranger? Since the man you come from
is a friend, I'm sure your news is friendly too.

OLD SERVANT

Orestes: he is dead. That's it in brief.

ELECTRA

Ah no! This day must mean the end for me.

CLYTEMNESTRA

What's this you say, what's this?
Speak, stranger. Pay her no attention.

OLD SERVANT

I've said, and say again: Orestes, he is dead.

ELECTRA

Catastrophe! My life is finished.

CLYTEMNESTRA

(*to Electra*) Look after your own problems, you.
(*to the old servant*) But tell me, stranger, tell me true:
how did he meet his end?

OLD SERVANT

That's why I have been sent, and I shall tell you all. 680
That man arrived to join
the glorious showpiece of the Greeks at Delphi
so that he could enter for the Pythian Games.
And when he heard the running-race announced
—the first to be decided—he entered it,
magnificent, admired by all those there.

He reached the finish of the course
in style to match his fine physique,
and came off with the victor's crown.
To sum up much in brief, I've never witnessed
strength and feats the like of his.
For certain every time the judge announced a winner, 690
[for running, double-track, pentathlon, as established°]
he took off the prize, congratulated for his victories.
This was the declaration naming him:°
'Orestes, Argive, son of Agamemnon,
who once led the famous army of the Greeks.'
And that is how it was . . . but when a god decides
to strike, no human's strong enough to get away.
°When on the final day the time arose, at dawn,
to mount the contest for the swiftest team of horses,
there he entered with the other charioteers. 700
°One was Achaean; one from Sparta;
there were two from Libya, expert four-horse racers;
fifth was one from Thessaly;
the next with brindled mares was from Aetolia;
the seventh from Magnesia;
the eighth from Aenia—white steeds;
the ninth from Athens, founded by the gods;
one from Boeotia was the tenth to mount his chariot.
Each took position in the place allotted by the judges. 710
Then the trumpet's blast of bronze—and they were off!
Together they all shouted to their teams and shook the reins;
the stadium resounded with the thundering of chariots,
and dust rose up in clouds.
All jostling for place they used their goads unsparingly,
flat out to overhaul each other's chariot-hubs
and snorting horses, whose fierce breath threw
flecks of foam upon their backs and whirling wheels.° (719)
And up till now the charioteers had all kept straight on course, (723)
but then the Aenian horses made a violent swerve
as they were turning from the sixth lap to the seventh,
crashing head-on with the team from Barce.°
Then one upon another they piled up, colliding,
till the Delphi race-course was all strewn with wreckage. 730

The skilful charioteer from Athens saw ahead,
and pulled aside in order to avoid
the surge of horses seething in mid-track.
Orestes had been holding back, behind the field,
relying on his final turn of speed;
but when he saw that he was left with just one other team,
he called out sharply to his horses
and set off in swift pursuit.
The two drew neck-and-neck; now one
and then the other would get just a head in front. 740
Through all the other circuits the poor man
had kept on steady with his chariot straight;
and as he went around the turning-post at either end (720)
he would just graze his axle-tip by letting loose
the right-hand horse and holding in the left. (722)
But then as he came round the final turn
he tightened up° the left-hand horse too much
and accidentally struck the corner of the post.
The axle-rod was snapped in two,
and he was thrown across the chariot rail and out.
And as fell upon the ground, all tangled
in the reins wrapped round himself,°
his horses went careering down the track.
The crowd there, when they saw him fallen
from his chariot, all cried aloud in pity 750
for the youth who'd had such triumphs,
only then to come to such a dreadful end.
Now he was dragged along the ground,
and sometimes tossed up in the air feet first,
until at last the other charioteers
just managed to restrain the horses.
They disentangled him, a mass of blood,
so battered even those most dear to him°
would not have recognized his mangled shape.
Immediately they burnt him on a funeral pyre,
and turned his mighty body
into paltry ashes in a small bronze urn.
Some chosen men from Phocis are conveying that,
so he may gain his lot of burial in his native land. 760

Well, that's what happened—
things bad enough when put in words:
for those of us who witnessed the event,
it was the most appalling thing I've ever seen.

CHORUS-LEADER

Dreadful! It seems the whole stock
of our royal dynasty is rooted out. . . .

CLYTEMNESTRA

What's this? O Zeus, am I to call this
happy news—or terrible, however positive?
It's bitter if the way to saving my own life
is through my own distress.

OLD SERVANT

What is it, lady, so dismays you in this news?

CLYTEMNESTRA

It is a powerful bonding, to give birth. 770
Impossible to hate your children,
even when they have ill-treated you.

OLD SERVANT

It seems my coming here has been no good.

CLYTEMNESTRA

No, not at all: how can you say 'no good',
when you have brought me certain proof that he is dead—
the one who, though deriving life from me,
then spurned my breast and care,
and went to live an alienated exile?
And me, once he had left this land, he never saw again;
yet he denounced me for his father's death,
and made such dreadful threats
that sleep would never sweetly wrap me round 780
by night or day, but every minute passed for me
as though I was about to meet my death.
But now . . . this very day releases me from fear of him—
(*turning to Electra*) and fear of this one too, since she
inside my house has been an even greater plague,
for ever draining dry my very blood of life.

But now, for all her threats, we shall be able
to live out our days secure in peace.

ELECTRA

How terrible, Orestes,
now that we must mourn your fate,
when you are treated with contempt 790
by your own mother here! Is that not fine?

CLYTEMNESTRA

Not fine for you. But as for him, he's fine all right.

ELECTRA

O Nemesis,° I call on you!
Hear how she speaks of him when he is newly dead.

CLYTEMNESTRA

She listened to the one she should, and she decided well.

ELECTRA

Yes, revel in it. You've struck lucky just for now.

CLYTEMNESTRA

You and Orestes cannot put a stop to this?

ELECTRA

We have been stopped—far from our stopping you.

CLYTEMNESTRA (*to the old man*)

Your coming, stranger, would be worth a lot,
if you have stopped her loud-mouthed ranting.

OLD SERVANT

If all is settled well, should I be on my way?

CLYTEMNESTRA

No, not at all. You then would not be treated properly by me, 800
nor worthy of the friend who sent you here.
Please come inside.
Leave her out here to howl about how terrible
things are for her and for her friends.

They go inside, leaving Electra by herself.

ELECTRA

So did the wretched woman
show her grief and anguish?

Did she weep with bitter tears, lament her son
who's met his death like this?
Oh no, she's gone, and laughing.
Dearest Orestes, by your death you've killed me too,
because you've torn out from my heart
the only hopes that I had left: 810
that you would live to come one day
and claim due vengeance for your father—and for me.
Now where am I to turn?
I'm all alone, bereft of you and of my father.
Now I have to act the slave again,
in service to the people that I most detest.
[my father's killers. So is all well with me?°]
This I declare: I never more shall share
a roof with them, not ever. I shall lie down friendless
by this doorway here, and waste my life away.
If any of those people there inside
becomes incensed by this, then let them kill me. 820
It will be a favour if I die, a misery if I live—
I've no desire for life.

LYRIC DIALOGUE LAMENT

CHORUS

°Where is the thunderbolt of Zeus
or the shining Sun,
if they can blithely watch these things,
yet not have them shown?

ELECTRA

(*cry of grief*)

CHORUS

What grief, dear child?

ELECTRA

(*cry of grief*)

CHORUS

Say nothing rash.

ELECTRA

You'll be my death.

CHORUS

How do you mean? 830

ELECTRA

If you hold out some hope for those
clearly dead and gone,
you will trample on me more,
when I'm crushed and down.

CHORUS

°Amphiaraus' story tells
how a chain of gold,
a female bribe, led to his tomb;
and yet underground . . .

ELECTRA

(*cry of grief*) 840

CHORUS

. . . he's strong, aware.

ELECTRA

(*cry of grief*)

CHORUS

His murderess . . .

ELECTRA

. . . herself was killed.

CHORUS

That's true indeed.

ELECTRA

I know, yes, for his grief
an avenger came.
But the one there was for me
is dead, snatched away.

CHORUS

You meet yet more misfortune.

ELECTRA

I know, I know too well— 850

my whole life is a torrent
that floods the whole year through
full of hateful horror.

CHORUS

We've seen what you mourn for.

ELECTRA

Then do not still attempt
to raise hopes of my brother
because all help from him
is now past and over.

CHORUS

Death comes to every mortal. 860

ELECTRA

But to fall beneath the hooves
of bolting horses, jabbing,
entangled with cruel death
in the reins that dragged him!

CHORUS

Unthinkable the torment.

ELECTRA

His body in an alien land
without me to adorn him
with my hands; and deprived of us
to bury and to mourn him. 870

SCENE 7

Chrysothemis returns in haste from the tomb.

CHRYSOTHEMIS

I'm so excited that I've run here, dearest sister,
in my haste forgetting modesty:
I'm bringing joyful respite from the troubles
that you've been so long lamenting.

ELECTRA

And how could you have possibly discovered
any cure for my distress when there's no healing it?

CHRYSOTHEMIS

Orestes has arrived. Believe me:
he is clearly here—as clearly as you see me now.

ELECTRA

Are you a crazy fool? Or are you laughing at
your own misfortune, and at mine as well? 880

CHRYSOTHEMIS

By our ancestral hearth, I am not mocking you.
He's here, I'm telling you.

ELECTRA

Poor fool! Who have you heard this story from,
to make you over-ready to believe in it?

CHRYSOTHEMIS

I believe in it because I've seen clear evidence—
seen for myself, not heard from someone else.

ELECTRA

What have you seen that's so reliable?
What sight has lit this raging fire in you?

CHRYSOTHEMIS

Please listen to me; hear me out
before you judge if I am sensible or foolish. 890

ELECTRA

Well, talk away, if you enjoy that so.

CHRYSOTHEMIS

I'll tell you everything I've seen.
As soon as I came near our father's ancient tomb
I could see streams of milk, new poured-out,
running from the grave-mound top,
and varied flowers were scattered
round about the monument.
I was astonished at this sight, and looked around
to see if there was anyone nearby.
And when I found that all the area was quiet,

I ventured closer to the tomb, 900
and at the edge I found a new-cut lock of hair.
As soon as I saw that, a well-known image
flew into my mind from looking on this token—
dearest of all people, our Orestes.
I picked it up, avoiding any word that risked ill luck,
and yet my eyes were filled with tears of joy.
And now I'm sure, as sure as I was then,
this tribute came from him and no one else.
Who else could this have been apart from you and me?
I know it was not me—and not you either, 910
seeing that you may not leave this house,
not even to the temples of the gods, unpunished.
And it's not our mother's way to do things such as this—
nor could she have without our noticing.
And so Orestes must have made these offerings.
Take courage, then, dear sister:
people's fortunes do not always stay the same.
Things used to be all grim for us, but now perhaps
this very day will prove the guarantee of happy times.

ELECTRA

°How I've been pitying your stupidity. 920

CHRYSOTHEMIS

But why? Is what I've told you not good news?

ELECTRA

You've no idea how far your mind has gone astray.

CHRYSOTHEMIS

Do I not know what I saw clearly, then?

ELECTRA

He's dead.
Your hopes of rescue thanks to him are gone.
Don't look to him for help.

CHRYSOTHEMIS

No, no! Who have you heard this from?

ELECTRA

From someone who was nearby when he died.

CHRYSOTHEMIS
Where is this man? How shock is coming over me.

ELECTRA
He's in the house—and more than welcome to our mother.

CHRYSOTHEMIS
Then all those offerings at our father's grave-mound— 930
who on earth could possibly have put them there?

ELECTRA
It's likely, I suppose, that someone laid them there
in memory of Orestes.

CHRYSOTHEMIS
What misery! And I was hurrying here with joyful news,
and had no notion of the depth of our disaster.
But, now that I've arrived, I find
all our old troubles and yet more as well.

ELECTRA
Well, that is how things are.
But if you follow what I say you'll make
the burden of our present agony less crushing.

CHRYSOTHEMIS
So can I make the dead stand up again? 940

ELECTRA
I don't mean that—I'm not so foolish.

CHRYSOTHEMIS
What are you urging me to do that's in my power?

ELECTRA
Nothing prospers without pain and toil, remember.

CHRYSOTHEMIS
I do; I'll share the burden with my utmost strength.

ELECTRA
Then listen to the thing I am resolved to carry through.
You're well aware we have no friends to call upon,
since Death has stripped us, and we two alone are left. 950
So long as I kept hearing that our brother was alive and well,

I held to hopes he would one day come here
to claim the debt of vengeance for our father.
But now that he is dead, I turn to you to join
with me, your sister, and not flinch from killing
the assassin of our father—
yes, Aegisthus.
I must keep nothing hidden from you any more.
What hope can you see still in prospect
while you wait around inactive?
You can complain of being robbed of your ancestral wealth; 960
you can be sad that for so long you have been
growing older with no wedding and no husband.
And don't imagine you will ever get these things:
Aegisthus is not such a fool
that he will ever let us, you or me, have children,
who would pose an obvious threat to him.
But if you'll follow what I say,
then first you shall show reverence for our father,
and our brother too; and then you'll be
for ever recognized as free by birth, 970
and so you'll win a worthy husband,
since everyone admires the sight of bravery.
Surely you can see the glory you'll attract
for both of us by following my plan.
For all who see us, friend or stranger,
shall acknowledge us with praise like this:
'Look, friend, that is the pair of sisters
who maintained their father's heritage,
and, though their enemies were strongly placed,
still risked their lives to have his death avenged. 980
We all should love them, reverence them,
and honour them with public celebration of their bravery!'
That kind of thing's what everyone will say, and we shall have
undying glory, both in life and death.
So, dearest sister, listen: work strong with your father;
labour with your brother; put an end
to all our troubles, yours as well as mine.
And recognize this truth: that for those nobly born
to live on in disgrace is true disgrace.

CHORUS-LEADER

In matters such as this it helps for both the speaker 990
and the listener to think ahead.

CHRYSOTHEMIS

Before she spoke, dear women, if she'd had good sense,
she would have exercised due caution—
which she has not done.
(*to Electra*) What have you in your sights,
the way you take up arms so recklessly,
and call on my support?
Can you not see you are a woman not a man,
and physically weaker than your enemies?
Their run of luck increases every day,
while ours recedes and comes to nothing. 1000
Who can plan to kill a man in that position,
and still hope to get away scot-free?
Look out you don't make bad things even worse
if someone overhears these words of yours.
It does for us no good if we achieve a fine repute,
but die an ignominious death.
[It is not death itself that's worst, but when you seek
for death, yet don't have power to make it sure.°]
So my response is this: before we're utterly destroyed 1010
and leave our dynasty obliterated,
hold your anger back.
I'll make quite sure that what you've said
remains as though unsaid and with no consequence.
And you at last should learn some sense,
and when you've got no strength,
give way before the ones who hold the power.

CHORUS-LEADER

Just pay attention to her. Nothing brings us humans
greater benefit than foresight and a mind that's wise.

ELECTRA

All you said was just as I expected:
I knew that you would cast aside what I proposed.
In that case I am going to have to do the deed
all by myself. I am not going to let it merely drop. 1020

CHRYSOTHEMIS
Well, well! If only you had been so purposeful the day
our father died, you would have changed it all!

ELECTRA
I was the same in spirit, but less understanding then.

CHRYSOTHEMIS
Well, try to keep that understanding all through life.

ELECTRA
I see this tone means you'll not act with me.

CHRYSOTHEMIS
Because this plan is likely to end up disastrously.

ELECTRA
I admire your prudence, but detest your cowardice.

CHRYSOTHEMIS
I hear your words, and then I shall accept approval too.

ELECTRA
Don't worry, that you'll never have from me.

CHRYSOTHEMIS
There's still a lot of time for judging that. 1030

ELECTRA
Now go away. In you there's no capacity to help.

CHRYSOTHEMIS
There is; but you have no capacity to learn.

ELECTRA
So go and tell your mother all of this.

CHRYSOTHEMIS
I won't: I harbour no such vicious hate for you.

ELECTRA
But see how much you are demeaning me.

CHRYSOTHEMIS
No not demeaning: thinking of your longer good.

ELECTRA
Which means I've got to follow your idea of what is right?

CHRYSOTHEMIS
Yes, show good sense; and then be the leader for us both.

ELECTRA

It's bad enough you speak so well, yet are so wrong.

CHRYSOTHEMIS

You've just described what's wrong with you. 1040

ELECTRA

D'you really not believe that what I say is right?

CHRYSOTHEMIS

Yet there are times when what is right is fraught with harm.

ELECTRA

Well, I have no desire to live according to those rules.

CHRYSOTHEMIS

If you go through with this, you'll end up saying I was right.

ELECTRA

I shall go through with it—and undeterred by you.

CHRYSOTHEMIS

You really will? And have no second thoughts?

ELECTRA

Because there's nothing worse than cowardly thoughts.

CHRYSOTHEMIS

It seems you do not understand a thing I say.

ELECTRA

I've long made up my mind—it's nothing new.

CHRYSOTHEMIS

°Well I am leaving in that case, 1050
since you can't bring yourself to like my words,
and I can't like the way that you behave.

ELECTRA

Then go on in. I'll never ever follow you—
no matter how much you may long for it.
Chasing after nothing is the height of foolishness.°

CHRYSOTHEMIS

If you believe that you are thinking right,
then think like that. But when you're deep in trouble,
then you'll come to praise my words.

Chrysothemis goes off into the house, leaving Electra.

THIRD CHORAL SONG

°Why, when we see the birds above
displaying such good sense,
supporting those they owe their life, 1060
with care and sustenance,
why do we not repay like them?
By Themis° who rights wrong,
and by great Zeus's lightning-bolt,
redress won't wait for long.
Send this appeal down to the dead
beneath to hear its voice:
tell Agamemnon that he bears
cacophonous disgrace.

Tell him the house is ill; the life 1070
of harmony is lost
between the sisters, unresolved.
Electra's left storm-tossed;
deserted, all alone she mourns
her father ceaselessly,
most like the plangent nightingale,
and views death fearlessly.
She is prepared to die if she
can put those two to death, 1080
the demon pair.° Who could match her
nobility of birth?

Nobody who's noble
would ever wish for shame,
cowardly behaviour
erasing their good name.
So you have rejected
a life submerged in tears,
and armed yourself to carry
off a double praise—
at one stroke a daughter
both supreme and wise.

We wish you wealth and power 1090
surpassing those you hate
as high as now you're low
downtrodden by their feet.
I've found you suffering under
deep misfortune's curse,
and yet observing truly
the great eternal laws,
and winning highest glory
through reverence for Zeus.

SCENE 8

°*Orestes and Pylades enter from the tomb direction carrying a bronze urn.*

ORESTES (*to chorus*)
Please tell us, women, whether we were rightly told
this is the way to where we want to go.

CHORUS-LEADER
What are you looking for? What brings you here? 1100

ORESTES
We have been seeking for the place Aegisthus lives.

CHORUS-LEADER
Your guide was faultless then: you have arrived.

ORESTES
Then one of you please let them know inside
that we, the people they've desired, have now arrived.

CHORUS-LEADER (*indicating Electra*)
This woman is the closest relative, and should announce it.

ORESTES
Then, lady, will you go inside, and say that men
from Phocis are here looking for Aegisthus.

ELECTRA
O misery! You don't mean you are bringing
actual proof of what we've heard reported?

ORESTES

I don't know anything about your story; 1110
but old Strophius has told me to bring news about Orestes.

ELECTRA

What message, stranger? Dread floods over me.

ORESTES

Inside a little urn we bring the dead man's
sparse remains, as you can see.

ELECTRA

Misery for me. So that is it. It's clear.
And this must be the burden that you bring.

ORESTES

If you are weeping for unfortunate Orestes,
then yes, this urn here houses all that's left of him.

ELECTRA

O stranger, by the gods I beg of you, please put it in my hands.
If this jar holds him, give it here to me, 1120
so I can weep, lamenting for myself
and all my family along with this poor ash.

ORESTES

Give it. Whoever she may be,
she can't be asking this with malice,
but she has to be a friend, or relative by blood.

ELECTRA (*taking the urn*)

O last memorial of the life
which was for me the dearest in the world,
last vestige of Orestes!
I receive you back with hopes so different
from those with which I sent you off.
For now I cup you in my hands, a nothingness;
but then, when I sent you from home,
you were so splendid, darling boy. 1130
O how I wish that I had died
before I rescued you from being killed,
and sheltered you within these arms of mine
to send you to a foreign land.
If you had lain in death that very day,

you would have shared a place in our ancestral tomb:
instead you met your wretched end
away from home, an exile in another land,
far separated from your sister.
And so I could not wash and dress your body
with my caring hands,
nor, as is proper, lift the sad weight
of your ashes from the glowing pyre. 1140
No, you were gathered by a stranger's hands,
and have come home,
a petty heap within a petty jar.
I think of all the care I took for you back then—
and all for nothing—often lavished on you
labour that I felt was sweet.
You never were your mother's boy,
not half so much as mine;
and no one in the house was nurse to you but me;
and you would always call me 'sister'.
Now in just one day all that
has disappeared along with you in death. 1150
You have, like some fierce whirlwind,
snatched it all away:
our father's gone;
I've died because of you;
and you are dead and lost.
Our enemies exult; our mother—no real mother—
is delirious with joy.
Yes her—you often sent me secret messages
to say how you would come
and take revenge on her yourself.
But our bad fortune, yours and mine, has taken
all of that, and sent you to me in this form:
instead of your dear flesh and blood,
this ash and futile shadow.
Ah, ah! So pitiful your body! 1160
Sent on such a dreadful journey!
Ah! You have destroyed me, dearest,
brought destruction on me, brother.
So now please let me in,

receive me into this, your home,
the nothing-me into your nothing-place,
so I may dwell with you below for all of time.
For when you were up here,
I used to share in everything with you;
and now I long to die,
so that I'll never be deprived
of being with you, even in the grave.
[for I see the dead are subject to no pain°] 1170

CHORUS-LEADER
Electra, think: you had a mortal father,
and Orestes, he was mortal too.
No use to mourn excessively,
for all of us are bound to pay this debt.

ORESTES (*who has been watching with growing unease*)
Ah, what should I say? I'm at a loss for words. . . .
I cannot keep control of how I speak.

ELECTRA
What is this troubling you? Why speak like that?

ORESTES
Is this the famous° person of Electra? Is this you?

ELECTRA
Yes, this is her—and in a wretched state.

ORESTES
What terrible misfortune!

ELECTRA
It can't be me you're pitying, stranger? 1180

ORESTES
This body so humiliated and mistreated.

ELECTRA
Your shocking words fit no one else but me.

ORESTES
To live in such a wretched and unmarried state.

ELECTRA
Why, stranger, do you stare at me and grieve like this?

ORESTES
How little have I been aware of my own sorrows.

ELECTRA
What has been said that prompts these thoughts?

ORESTES
My seeing you beset by so much suffering.

ELECTRA
Yet only few of all my pains are visible.

ORESTES
How could there be things yet more horrible to see?

ELECTRA
The way that I am housed with murderers. 1190

ORESTES
Whose murderers? What wrong is this you're pointing to?

ELECTRA
My father's. And I am enslaved to them by force.

ORESTES
Who is it that imposes this strict rule on you?

ELECTRA
She's called my mother, but she's nothing like a mother.

ORESTES
What does she do? Use violence? Make life harsh?

ELECTRA
She uses force, she makes life hard, and every wrong.

ORESTES
And is there nobody to help or put a stop to this?

ELECTRA
Not one. You've brought the ashes of the one there was.

ORESTES
Poor woman, I've been filled with pity as I look on you.

ELECTRA
Well, you're the only one who's ever pitied me. 1200

ORESTES
Because I am the only one who's come to share your pain.

ELECTRA
You cannot, can you, be some sort of relative of mine?

ORESTES (*indicating the chorus*)
I can be open only if these women here are friends.

ELECTRA
Yes, they are friends—you can depend on them.

ORESTES
Give back this urn, and then you can know everything.

Orestes takes hold of the urn, but Electra will not let go.

ELECTRA
Ah, by the gods I beg you, stranger, don't do that to me.

ORESTES
Do as I say, and you shall not go wrong.

ELECTRA
No, I implore you, do not take away the dearest thing I have.

ORESTES
I tell you, let it go.

ELECTRA
O how I grieve for you, Orestes,
if I'm to be deprived of even burying you. 1210

ORESTES
Don't say unlucky words—you've no good reason to lament.

ELECTRA
What? No good reason to lament for my own brother?

ORESTES
That kind of language does not fit the situation.

ELECTRA
Am I to be deprived of my due rights towards the dead?

ORESTES
You are deprived of nothing. This is not for you.

ELECTRA
It is, though, if it is Orestes' body I am clasping here.

ORESTES
It's not Orestes' body—it's been dressed up with words.

ELECTRA

Then where's that poor man's final burial place?

ORESTES

It's nowhere—since the living have no burial.

ELECTRA

°What are you saying, boy? 1220

ORESTES

I'm telling you no lies.

ELECTRA

You mean the man's alive?

ORESTES

If I have breath myself.

ELECTRA

You mean you're him?

ORESTES (*showing a ring on his hand*)

See here our father's signet seal—
and now decide if what I say rings true.

ELECTRA

Most welcome light of day!

ORESTES

Most welcome, I say yes to that.

ELECTRA

Your voice! You have arrived?

ORESTES

No need to call for any other.

They embrace.

ELECTRA

I have you in my arms?

ORESTES

And may you ever keep this hold of me.

ELECTRA (*to chorus*)

My dearest women of this city,
here you see Orestes:
he who died to carry out a scheming plan,
and now through scheming has been brought to life.

CHORUS-LEADER

We see him, daughter. And this happy turn 1230
has filled our eyes with tears of joy.

Part lyric, part spoken dialogue between Electra and Orestes.

ELECTRA

°Son of that man dearest,
you've arrived here clearly,
found me, seen me, held me,
her that you have yearned for.

ORESTES

Yes, I have come. But wait and make no noise.

ELECTRA

What do you mean?

ORESTES

It's better to stay quiet in case someone inside should hear.

ELECTRA

By Artemis the virgin,
I'd not trouble feeling 1240
fear of useless women
inside doing nothing.

ORESTES

Be careful! Women also can be deadly—
you have some experience of that, I think.

ELECTRA

Yes, you have reminded
me of dreadful evil,
never clouded over,
not to be forgotten. 1250

ORESTES

I know that too. But when the circumstances tell us,
that will be the time to recollect those deeds.

ELECTRA

All, all time in future
may let me express this

fully. But it's only
now I have the freedom.

ORESTES

I know; and so make sure you keep that freedom safe.

ELECTRA

By doing what?

ORESTES

Not speaking long when time's not right.

ELECTRA

Who could bear to stifle 1260
words and change to silence,
now I've seen your face here
past all expectation?

ORESTES

You've seen it was the gods who spurred me to return.

ELECTRA

You declare a blessing
that is overwhelming;
I see this homecoming
as the gods' endeavour. 1270

ORESTES

I am reluctant to restrain you from rejoicing,
but I fear you may be overcome with jubilation.

ELECTRA

After so long a time
you have made this journey.
Do not spoil my gladness;
after my ill-fortune,
don't begrudge the pleasure
of your face before me. . . .

ORESTES

I'd be angry if I saw that from another.

ELECTRA

So you agree? 1280

ORESTES

Of course I do.

ELECTRA

Your voice I've heard despite
every expectation,
but still restrained my cry,
quelling my elation.
But I embrace you now,
with your face so welcome,
that I could not forget
in my degradation.

ORESTES

Do not spend words beyond what is essential;
so don't tell me all about our mother's viciousness,
or how Aegisthus keeps on draining our ancestral wealth 1290
by dissipating it without a care,
since that would merely hold you back
from seizing on this opportunity.
Just tell us what will serve the present situation:
what we should reveal or what conceal
to suit our present quest: to put a stop
to all that laughter from our enemies.
And make quite sure that you don't let our mother
get suspicious when we've gone inside
by wearing a glad look upon your face.
Just keep on grieving as you would
had the catastrophe been truly and not falsely told.
Once that we have success, 1300
we'll then be free to celebrate and laugh at will.

ELECTRA

Dear brother, what you want is also good for me,
since I have got my joy from you and not myself;
so even if I'd found some great gain for myself,
I would not grasp it if it hurt you in the slightest way.
If I did that I'd not be doing service
to the guiding spirit of the moment.
You must have heard about the situation here:

Aegisthus is not now at home;
our mother, though, is here indoors.
And have no fear that she will ever see me 1310
with a happy face—my long-time hatred for her
has been etched too deeply into me.
And now I've seen you, I shall still not cease
from weeping tears—for how am I to stop
when, with this one arrival,
I have looked upon you
as both dead and as alive?
°You've had a strange effect on me,
so much that, if my father were to come before me,
I'd not think it fantasy,
but would believe I really saw him standing there.
So now you've come to me the way you have,
command me as you will.
Because, if I'd been left alone,
I would have made quite sure of one of these two things: 1320
either to survive in noble fashion
or else nobly face my death.

SCENE 8

CHORUS-LEADER

°I think you should keep quiet, as I can hear
some person coming from the house.

ELECTRA (*putting on an act*)

Please enter, strangers.
No one would desire to keep you here outdoors,
when you are bringing what you are,
however much it might distress them to receive it.

OLD SERVANT (*emerging in a hurry*)

You stupid thoughtless fools!
Do you not care about your lives?
Are you so lacking any sense that you don't realize
you're not just close to deadly danger 1330
but are deep caught up in it?

If I had not been keeping constant watch here by the door,
your doings would have got inside before you did—
but luckily for you I have been looking after this.
So now abandon all this talk, these endless cries of joy,
and get inside.
In situations of this kind delay is bad;
and it's high time to get it over with.

ORESTES
So what will things be like inside when I go in?

OLD SERVANT
They're good, since nobody will realize who you are. 1340

ORESTES
I take it you've reported that I'm dead?

OLD SERVANT
For them you are a dead man with the shades below.

ORESTES
And are they glad of this? What do they say?

OLD SERVANT
I'll tell you when it's over with.
For now, though, everything is fine with them,
including what is not.

ELECTRA (*intervening*)
Who is this, brother? Tell me, please.

ORESTES
Do you not recognize him?

ELECTRA
I don't understand.

ORESTES
Do you not know the man you gave me to back then?

ELECTRA
What are you saying? Who?

ORESTES
This is the one who, thanks to your precaution,
smuggled me away to Phocis. 1350

ELECTRA

What? This is him? The one and only person
I found loyal when our father had been killed?

ORESTES

This is the very one. No need ask me more.

ELECTRA

You dearest ray of light,
you single saviour of the house of Agamemnon,
how can it be you've come
—the very one who rescued him and me
from deepest danger?
Oh dearest hands, dear feet which served so well!
How could you have been there beside me for so long
and not been recognized, not obvious?
Instead you tortured me with words,
while knowing things that proved most sweet for me. 1360
So greetings, father!—for I see you as my father—
greetings! In one single day I have both hated you
the most of anyone, and loved you most as well.

OLD SERVANT

For now, I thank you.
As for what has passed between that time and now,
the many turning days and nights
shall make all clear to you, Electra.
(*turning to Orestes and Pylades*)
But you two standing here, I say to you:
now is the time to act;
now Clytemnestra is alone;
for now there are no men inside.
But think how, if you put this off, you'll have to fight 1370
with them and others more in number,
more experienced in fighting skill.

ORESTES

No call for further words, then;
Pylades, let's turn to action,
and immediately get inside,
as soon as we have greeted the ancestral gods
who have their place within this entrance-way.

Orestes, Pylades, and the old servant all go inside, taking the urn.

ELECTRA (*addressing the statue of Apollo*)
O lord Apollo, hear their prayers with favour,
and mine too—I who have often stood and offered you
whatever I could lay my hands upon.
And now, Apollo, taking what I have
I pray, I beg you, I implore: 1380
provide your ready help in carrying out this plan.
And that will show mankind what sort of recompense
the gods dispense for wickedness.

Electra follows them inside.

FOURTH CHORAL SONG

CHORUS
Ares° breathing blasts of blood
presses on inside;
those unrelenting hounds°
hunt down wicked deeds.
Visions that my mind can see
won't wait long to be. 1390

He's advanced to help the dead
with deceitful tread
into the ancestral seat
with blood-sharpened blade.
Hermes° guides the dark deceit
on, on—no long wait.

SCENE 9

Electra comes back outside by herself.

ELECTRA
Dear women, soon they will be carrying out
the deed. But stay here quiet.

CHORUS
What are they doing at this moment? 1400

ELECTRA
She's decorating round the funeral urn,
while they stand close beside her.

CHORUS
And why have you come hurrying out?

ELECTRA
To keep watch and make sure
Aegisthus does not come upon us by surprise.

CLYTEMNESTRA (*calling from inside*)
O help! This building is deserted
by our friends and full of murderers.

ELECTRA
A cry from somebody° inside!
Did you not hear it, friends?

CHORUS
Excruciating, yes I did—
it makes me shake with dread!

CLYTEMNESTRA (*from inside*)
Ah! No! Aegisthus, where, where can you be?

ELECTRA
And there is someone calling out again! 1410

CLYTEMNESTRA (*from inside*)
My child, my son, take pity on your mother!

ELECTRA
He got no pity, though, from you—
and neither did his father.

CHORUS
O city, dynasty of pain,
your daily fate is in decline!

CLYTEMNESTRA (*from inside*)
Ah, ah! I'm stabbed!

ELECTRA
Be strong: strike twice as hard!°

CLYTEMNESTRA (*from inside*)
Ah, stabbed again!

ELECTRA
If only that could be Aegisthus too!

CHORUS
The curses now begin their work;°
the dead below the ground awake.
The killers' blood flows back in flood, 1420
to be drained down by those long dead.

Enter Orestes and Pylades from the door, with bloody hands.

CHORUS-LEADER
And here they are, hands dripping with the blood
of violent sacrifice. Yet I do not condemn.

ELECTRA
Orestes, how go things?

ORESTES
All good inside the house,
provided that Apollo gave us good advice.

ELECTRA
The wretch is dead then?

ORESTES
You need no longer fear humiliation
from your mother's cruelty.

°<*three or four brief lines missing around here*>

CHORUS
Stop now, because I can see clear
that there's Aegisthus coming into view.

ELECTRA
Quick, boys, get back inside! 1430

ORESTES
Where do you see the man?

ELECTRA
He is approaching from the outskirts—jauntily.

CHORUS

Get back inside, quick as you may:
you have done well, so now do more.

ORESTES

Don't worry, we'll complete the job.

ELECTRA

Then hurry where you plan to go.

ORESTES

Yes, on my way.

They quickly go back in.

ELECTRA

Leave things out here to me.

CHORUS

It would be good for you to pour
soothing words into his ear,
and then he'll hurry in to face 1440
the ambush Justice sets in place.

SCENE 10

Enter Aegisthus briskly from the city direction.

AEGISTHUS

So, which of you can tell me where these Phocians are?
They have reported, so I gather, that Orestes
met his end caught in the wreckage of his chariot.
(*seeing Electra*) Ah, you! Yes, I'll ask you,
the woman who till now showed such defiance—
this must affect you most,
and so you will be best informed.

ELECTRA

Of course I know, since otherwise I'd be untouched
by what has happened to my dearest kin.

AEGISTHUS

Where are these strangers then? —just tell me that. 1450

ELECTRA
Inside, where they have found a genial host.

AEGISTHUS
And did they really tell how he is dead?

ELECTRA
They did not only say: they showed it in the flesh.

AEGISTHUS
So I can see, and witness it for sure?

ELECTRA
Yes, you can see. It makes a most unenviable sight.°

AEGISTHUS
Your words have given me unusual delight!

ELECTRA
Take pleasure then, if you are really pleased at this.

AEGISTHUS (*commanding*)
Now open up the doors I say,
so that the Myceneans and the Argives all
can see what is revealed.
And anyone who has been pinning empty hopes 1460
upon this man can look upon his corpse.
And after that they should accept my bridle,
and not wait until it takes hard punishment
to make them sensible.

°*Electra opens the stage-doors, and a covered bier with two men [Orestes and Pylades] standing by is revealed.*

ELECTRA
There! I have done as you command.
With time I've learnt it's best to join the stronger side.

AEGISTHUS
O Zeus, I see a vision here that's come about
through some divine resentment—
though whether with their righteous anger too I cannot say.°
(*to the man by the bier*)
Now draw the covering from his face
so that I too may give my kin due lamentation.

ORESTES

You lift it for yourself. It is for you, not me, 1470
to look upon this sight and offer some fond words.

AEGISTHUS

That's good advice that I accept.
(*to the man*) And you, go summon Clytemnestra here,
if she is somewhere in the house.

ORESTES (*as Aegisthus draws back to the covering*)

She is already near to you.
No need to look elsewhere.

AEGISTHUS

Ah, what is this I see?

ORESTES

Afraid? Who of? Who don't you recognize?°

AEGISTHUS

Who are these men? I've fallen right into their trap.

ORESTES

Do you not realize that you, still living,
have been holding conversation with the dead?

AEGISTHUS

Ah yes, I understand your meaning.
This man who's speaking with me here 1480
can be no other than Orestes.

ORESTES

So good at prophecy, and yet so long mistaken!

AEGISTHUS

I'm a dead man, I can see.
Yet let me say just one small thing.

ELECTRA

For god's sake, brother, don't allow him
any time to talk or go on making speeches,.
[When people are mixed deep in troubles,
how can the one about to die
get any benefit from winning further time?°]
No, kill him quick.

And after killing him, consign him to the buriers
who are right for him,° well out of sight from us.
For me this is the only way for him
to make amends for all his past of wrongs. 1490

ORESTES (*to Aegisthus*)
You get inside and quick about it.
This contest is not one of words: it's for your life.

AEGISTHUS
Why are you taking me indoors?
What need of darkness if this deed is good?
Why are you not prepared to strike right here?

ORESTES
Don't tell me what to do.
Go in to where you killed my father,
so you die in that same place.

AEGISTHUS
Is it inevitable that this house should witness
all the horrors of the dynasty of Pelops,
both those present and to come?°

ORESTES
Well yours at least.
I am an expert prophet of this much.

AEGISTHUS
Your father could not claim to have such skill! 1500

ORESTES
A lot of answering back, while your departure
gets delayed. Go in.

AEGISTHUS
You lead.

ORESTES
No, you must go in front.

AEGISTHUS
Afraid I might escape from you?

ORESTES
I don't want you to die with any sweetening:
I want to make quite sure it's sour.

[This punishment should fall upon all those
who want to act outside the laws: yes, death.
Then criminality would not be rife.°]

Aegisthus is forced inside by Orestes and Pylades, followed by Electra.

CHORUS

So, you dynasty of Atreus,
you've emerged from tribulations,
struggling into liberation,
ended with this present action.° 1510

The chorus depart towards the city.

EXPLANATORY NOTES

Note that line numbers refer to the standard numbering of the Greek texts, not to the lines of this translation.

ANTIGONE

1 ff. [*SD*] *Antigone and Ismene* . . . : the two young women come out of the gates of the house, something they should not normally do without permission or supervision. This is emphasized by Antigone at line 18 where 'beyond the outer doors' indicates the front gates that lead out from the central courtyard of the house.

1 *My sister*: Antigone puts an immediate emphasis on blood-kinship, which is her driving motivation. Later, though, at the end of the prologue and then in lines 537 ff. she rejects Ismene as unworthy of her sisterhood.

8 *the Commander*: Antigone's first allusion to Creon does not name him. He himself and everyone else refers to him as the new 'king' (*basileus*), but Antigone only allows him his military authority.

11 ff. *I've heard of nothing* . . . : Ismene summarizes the immediate 'back-story', that the invasion by the Seven has been driven off, and that in the battle the two sons of Oedipus killed each other. This will be further evoked by the chorus in their first lyric.

32 *and me, yes me*: this initiates an emphasis by Antigone on her own will, brought out by repeated first-person pronouns: see lines 45, 48, 71, 80.

36 *public stoning*: stoning is generally a communally undertaken punishment, through which no individual is specified as the killer. So Creon is later unable to enforce this.

50 ff. *Just think of how* . . . : again Ismene gives a résumé of the story going further in the past. It closely matches *Oedipus the King* (most probably a later play) except for the death of Oedipus.

73 *beloved I shall lie* . . . *beloved*: Antigone links herself with her brother so closely that it is hard to avoid the thought that there is a hint of incestuous love here (even though posthumous)—see also p. 10. And this incest, unlike that of her father and mother, is deliberate. That uncomfortable evocation is sustained rather than contradicted by her striking oxymoron: what she proposes is both perverse and holy.

74–6 *I have to please* . . . *evermore*: the Greeks did not have any clear or generally accepted picture of 'life' in the underworld. Antigone is confident that she will spend eternity in close and affectionate company with her family, but, while this notion is common in Christian eschatology, it would not strike Sophocles' audience as unquestionable—see further p. 11.

99 [*SD*] *Ismene goes* . . . : the sisters came on together, but here they part ways. Ismene goes back indoors to women's territory, while Antigone sets off alone towards the world of men and of battle. At the same juncture the chorus of elders arrive from the third direction, that of the city.

100 ff. [*First Choral Song*]: the chorus is made up of elders of the city, *gerontes*, as they identify themselves at line 159. They have been summoned to meet here by Creon, as Antigone has already indicated (33–4). These patriotic old men sing in celebration of the defeat of the army raised to attack Thebes by Polynices, addressing a string of favourable deities, beginning with Sun. They bring in several of the leading national emblems or landmarks of Thebes, including the famous seven gates in the mighty walls (101, 141) and the river Dirce (104). The song consists of four stanzas, arranged in two pairs; and at the end of each stanza, there are some chanted lines in the anapaestic metre.

106–7 *You reversed* . . . *battle gear*: there are textual problems here. In the interests of clarity this translation omits a reference to 'white shield' (106) and later to 'white feather' (114), both apparently symbols of the Argive army.

111 *doubtful quarrels*: this plays on the name of Polynices, which might be taken to mean 'of many disputes'.

117–26 *So above our homes* . . . *Theban snake*: the Argive invaders are envisaged as a kind of eagle-monster, which is driven back by the snake or dragon which stands for Thebes. Some obscurities in lines 118–19, 122–3 have been pruned.

131–8 *hurling down the one* . . . *falls and fails*: the chorus claim that the arrogance of the invading army offended Zeus. They single out Capaneus, so notorious that he does not need to be named; he climbed the wall with a flaming torch, and made blasphemous boasts.

139 *Ares*: the war god had local associations with Thebes.

141–2 *Seven leaders* . . . *face each other*: the story was that one of each of the seven leaders of the army, including Polynices, took his stand at one of the gates. In Aeschylus' *Seven against Thebes* there is a scene where Eteocles selects a Theban defender for each gate, with himself at the seventh.

143 *Zeus of trophies*: the custom was for the victors to set up a frame decked with the arms of the defeated.

149 *chariot-famous Thebes*: the reference to chariots here and in Antigone's lament at line 845 may allude obliquely to the city's success in pan-Hellenic chariot races, as celebrated by the Theban poet, Pindar.

154 *Bacchus*: a title of Dionysus, whose mother was the daughter of Cadmus, founder of Thebes. He was an important patron god of the city.

155 ff. [*SD*] *Creon* . . . *the palace*: it is significant that Creon comes from the palace, not the battlefield. He has taken over the royal power, as the closest to the now extinct male line of succession from Laius.

174 *my close kinship*: Creon has emphasized the royal line, but his kinship lies, in fact, in his being the brother of Iocasta. There is not, however, any suggestion of a rival claim.

187 *my country's enemy as kin to me*: this poses the nub of Creon's fundamental disagreement with Antigone over the essence of who counts as a *philos* (friend, dear one, kin, one's own). For her the tie of blood outweighs all other claims: for Creon it is the interests of the city (in modern terms the country or nation) that are paramount.

223 ff. *My lord . . .* : the guard presents an unusual vignette for Greek tragedy. He is a common soldier who has news to report, but he is also garrulous and argumentative, given to amusing quips. The nearest parallel is probably the old Corinthian shepherd in *Oedipus the King*, but he is less persistently 'cheeky'. When Creon has been so grand and sententious, the guard does to some extent deflate his officiousness. It is an interesting question whether this makes Creon come across as more or less humanly approachable or vulnerable.

248 *What man . . .* : Creon, who always tends to suspect mercenary motives (see lines 221–2, 293 ff.), assumes that the culprit must be a man; and that he is part of a conspiracy (289 ff., 325).

255 ff. *The corpse . . .* : the body has not been moved, let alone buried, but something has been done to cover it from exposure. While the guard thinks this might have been done by some passer-by ('as though performed by someone to avoid pollution'), Antigone's act was, in fact, to save her brother from total deprivation of any dignity or honour after death.

295 ff. *There is no currency . . .* : Creon's tirade against taking corrupt payments verges on crude expression in places. (Lines 300–1 'money's opened up . . . without restraint' rather overload the denunciation, and might possibly have been added.)

309 *insolence*: the Greek word here is *hybris*. This word is not as clearly definable as its use in English supposes: it is a way of claiming, not necessarily rightly, that someone's behaviour is insultingly high-handed.

332 ff. [*Second Choral Song*]: this choral song, often known (rather misleadingly) as the 'Ode on Man', is one of the most celebrated in Greek poetry. The first three of its four stanzas catalogue varied examples of human achievement and civilization, both technical and social. It is only in the last stanza that the potential for wrong-doing is also raised, apparently referring to the defiance against Creon's edict. The twist is that the person they think of as so objectionably anti-social immediately turns out to be a young woman and of royal lineage.

332–3 *formidable . . . formidable*: the Greek word is *deinos* which covers a wide range of things that are out of the ordinary, ranging from the terrifying to the marvellous. Here its sense is clearly positive, but it should retain a hint of threat. ('Formidable' should be stressed on the second syllable.)

370 *raise their city secure . . . no city*: this attempts to convey two juxtaposed Greek words made with the word '*polis*': *hypsipolis* (literally 'with high city') and *apolis* ('with no city').

415 ff. *Then suddenly a whirlwind . . .* : there is a suggestion of divine intervention in this sudden dust-storm; and it is unexplained how Antigone found her way to the body under those conditions. There is no good reason, however, to call on the gods to explain the way that the body gets buried twice. Antigone's first honouring of her brother's body has been undone by the actions of uncovering it, and that is why she has returned, and why she vehemently curses 'those who'd done this thing' (lines 427–8). It has been proposed that the first burial was 'in fact' done by Ismene, but this is to posit a kind of detective-story reconstruction which is completely inappropriate to a play of this kind.

450 ff. *I did . . .* : this celebrated speech has often been treated reverentially as some kind of moral and religious manifesto. It is, however, exclusively concerned with Antigone's particular defence of the emphasis she lays on the honour of the dead—see further p. 11. The point about 'unwritten statutes' is that, because they have not been publicly recorded, they can only be asserted not confirmed: the trouble with them is that they cannot be universally agreed because there is no empirical confirmation.

484–5 *she's the man*: Creon begins to reveal something of an obsession with gender-superiority.

486–7 *our household Zeus*: the cult of Zeus *herkeios* ('of the hurdles') was a family ritual observed within the courtyard of the house. This also brings Ismene and her recent strange behaviour into Creon's mind.

504–7 *all these people . . . what you please*: this introduces a significantly open question: does Creon, as he believes, speak for all the citizens? Does even the chorus agree? 'One-man rule' translates the Greek word *tyrannis*, which is not as negative as 'tyranny' because the extent to which this and related terms have a positive or negative sense in fifth-century Greek depends on context.

514 *support that view*: in this dialogue Antigone claims, as she always does, to know best what the dead feel and think.

523 *I'm bound by birth . . . enmity*: this line is sometimes treated as though it were some sort of precursor of a religion of universal love. But in context Antigone, who uses two unique verbs meaning something like 'co-love' and 'co-hate', is talking of the bonds of blood-kinship not of humanity as a whole. See further p. 10.

568–70 *your own son's bride . . . him and her*: this is the first allusion to the betrothal between Antigone and Creon's son Haemon. Although Creon's reply alludes to the Athenian marriage contract which spoke of 'the sowing of legitimate children', his dismissal of the match strikes a callous, even coarse, note. Ismene's reply in line 570 seems to imply a special affinity between Antigone and Haemon.

572 *Beloved Haemon . . .* : some editors have given this line to Antigone because of its exclamation of personal affection. But this would disrupt the dialogue between Ismene and Creon; and nowhere else in the play does Antigone ever express any feelings for Haemon. Her love has been entirely devoted to the dead.

583 ff. [*Third Choral Song*]: this song has at its base the theme of the disaster which strikes a family dogged by faults, but this is expressed in highly metaphorical, often enigmatic, terms. The key word *ate* (both vowels long), here rendered as 'disaster', recurs four times. This word reaches a range of dire experiences, from the psychological (blind misjudgement, craziness) to the physical (destruction, catastrophe).

594 *of this dynasty*: the Greek says 'the house of the Labdacids [descendants of Labdacus]'. Labdacus was the father of Laius, the father of Oedipus.

602 *the blade of the gods below*: a particularly tangled cluster of metaphors is capped by a textual question. Antigone must in some sense be the 'latest root' which brought the light of hope to the royal dynasty. But now that root has, according to the reading in the manuscripts, been harvested or cut by the 'bloody dust' (*konis*) of the gods below. I have accepted the emendation of *konis* to *kopis*, which means a cleaver, or here perhaps a scythe. Either way this is then glossed as 'foolish speech and thoughts beyond reason's reach'.

603 *thoughts beyond reason's reach*: literally 'Erinys of the mind'. An Erinys is a dangerous punishing god, usually translated as 'Fury'; but here the word is evidently figurative.

613–14 *nothing vast . . . without disaster*: the text and meaning here are very uncertain. What is clear is that some sort of excess or transgression against Zeus' law is bound to bring *ate* (see on 584).

619 *foot's smouldering*: 'walking on embers' was proverbial for risky behaviour.

626 ff. *Here comes Haemon, youngest . . .* : there were stories of an elder brother who had died recently in the war against the Seven—see on 1303. The chorus's introduction emphasizes Haemon's betrothal to Antigone, already raised by Ismene, but not by Antigone herself, at 568 ff. It is likely that line 628 was added to explain an unusual term that is used for fiancée.

658–9 '*blood-kin Zeus*': the epithet that Creon gives to Antigone's Zeus, *synhaimon* (literally 'of shared blood'), plays on Haemon's name.

663–7 *But someone . . . just and opposite alike*: the sequence of the argument makes much better sense if these five lines are shifted to come between lines 671 and 672, and most editors accept this transposition. If right, we don't know how the textual disruption happened.

667 *in matters great . . . opposite alike*: it is difficult to make sense of the text of the Greek in this line.

687 *but it may . . . a different way*: a rather obscure line that may have been a later addition.

690 ff. *You need to know* . . . : Haemon's account of what the people of the city are saying may be seen as a turning point in the play's portrayal of Creon: see further p. 8.

693–9 *the city's filled* . . . : the language that Haemon attributes to the people's assessment is that of heroic glory, like that aspired to by the great warriors of epic.

after 749 *Slave to a woman!* . . . : I am agreeing with editors who have argued that lines 756–7 fit into the sequence of argument better here than where they occur in the manuscripts.

773 ff. *I'll take her to a place* . . . : Creon's abandonment of the punishment by public stoning may tacitly recognize that he does not have popular support (see note on 36).

781 ff. [*Fourth Choral Song*]: the chorus, neglecting the ethical and political dimensions to Haemon's case, launch into a hymn to Desire (*Eros*), assuming that this must be what is driving his support for Antigone. It is this, they sing, that has stirred up the conflict between these two men 'of shared blood', again the use of *synhaimon*, playing on Haemon's name (see on 658–9).

781 *heart*: this translates a speculative emendation of a word in the text which, if left, would mean 'possessions'.

788–9 *defeats highest laws*: text and sense uncertain.

806–82 [*Lyric Dialogue*]: in this lament, as Antigone begins her final journey to her living tomb, she sings five stanzas. The chorus respond to the first two with chanted anapaests, and to the second two with brief emotional lyric. The dominant motifs are that Antigone's prison-chamber in the rock is both a bedroom and a tomb; and that instead of living to be married she will sleep with the dead. Acheron is a river to be crossed on the way to the underworld.

823–33 *I have heard how Niobe . . . takes me to bed*: Antigone likens her fate to a famous figure of myth who was encased in stone after death. Niobe (identified in the Greek as 'the Phrygian guest-woman, daughter of Tantalus') came from Asia Minor to Thebes to marry the king Amphion. Artemis and Apollo punished her for her boasts about her children by killing them all. The story was that she went back home, and grieved until she was turned into a rock on Mount Sipylus, near Sardis. Tourists were shown a rocky outcrop that was shaped like a woman's head and which had water trickling down its face.

834–8 *But she was divine . . in life and death*: the chorus insist that Niobe was different because her father, Tantalus, was the son of Zeus. They still try to comfort Antigone by going so far as to compare her with the divine; but Antigone finds this reservation offensive.

862 *dynasty*: the Greek says 'of the descendants of Labdacus'—see on 594.

870 *your burial*: the transmitted Greek says 'your marriage'. This would have to refer to Polynices' marriage to an Argive princess, which helped him to

raise the seven contingents against Thebes. I have preferred an emendation which puts all the emphasis on his death.

891–928 *My tomb . . .* : after her lyric Antigone has this last speech in which she laments her early death, but claiming that it is worth it in order to maintain her loyalty to her dead family. Her rightness, she maintains, shows up Creon's wrong. In the middle of this there is a strange digression in which she argues that it was a right 'principle' that she had to bury a brother, although the same obligation would not have applied to a husband or a child. Many critics have thought that the speech would be stronger without these lines (and Goethe, no less, hoped that a scholar might be able to show that they were not by Sophocles!). While some of the objections to them are weak, for example that they are irrational, or that they are inconsistent with her earlier self-justifications, there are nonetheless some serious problems which do make the authenticity of lines 905–12 open to question—see next note.

905–12 *Because if children . . . ever could be born*: although these lines were already in the text of Sophocles' play by the time of Aristotle a century later, I am nonetheless inclined to believe that they are an addition by an actor (or another playwright). Firstly, this is a kind of folk-tale argument used to save the life of a brother rather than an explanation to justify burying a brother after his death. This very motif is, in fact, found in the histories of Herodotus (3.119), where a Persian woman pleads with the King for the life of her brother. Furthermore the wording in the play is clearly based on the historian's version, which was published later, although it might have been in circulation earlier. It is anomalous that Antigone should employ such a specious argument in such an intense and moving context.

There are further problems. First the argument is introduced in line 905 by 'Because . . .' (*gar*), but what follows is in no way an explanation. Secondly she says she would not have buried anyone except a brother 'in defiance of the city's will' (907). This is the same phrase as was used by Ismene of Creon's decree in the prologue (79); yet Antigone's case, endorsed by Haemon, is that Creon's decree does *not* have the support of the citizens—in other words she did not do it 'in defiance of the city's will'. Thirdly she says (908) that the argument about the irreplaceability of a brother is a matter of a 'principle' (*nomos*). The same word then confusingly recurs a few lines later in 913–14, where it is the principle of burial, not of the special relationship of a brother, that is being maintained. Last, and least cogent, there is some rather contorted wording of a kind not characteristic of Sophocles in lines 905–6 and in 909–12, the passage that is most closely modelled on Herodotus.

944 ff. [*Fifth Choral Song*]: this choral song is cast as a kind of consolation for Antigone, even though she is not there to hear it. It evokes three myths, each with an oblique and different relation to the situation in her tragedy.

944–54 *Danae had to endure leaving* . . . : the first stanza concerns Danae, a princess of Argos, who was imprisoned in a tower by her father to prevent her from having a child. Zeus visited her in the form of a shower of gold, and the result was the hero Perseus. Despite this divine favour Danae's story was, like Antigone's, not a happy one.

955–65 *And Dionysus confined* . . . : the second tells of Lycurgus, the hot-tempered king of Thrace, who tried (like Pentheus at Thebes) to prevent the acceptance of the cult of Dionysus. Among his various harsh punishments, this verse concentrates on his being shut away in a cave. Clearly his story suggests parallels with Creon as well as Antigone.

966–87 *And at Thracian Salmydessus* . . . : the second pair of stanzas (which contain several serious textual problems) is devoted to a single myth. Phineus was king of Salmydessus at the entrance to the Black Sea not far from Byzantium. He married Cleopatra, born to Boreas, the North Wind, and a princess of Athens. They had two sons; but when Phineus divorced her and imprisoned her in order to remarry, his second wife blinded the two boys. There were various stories of what happened later, but the emphasis here is on the way that Cleopatra's high pedigree did not save her from a deeply unhappy life-story. The very last words in line 987 ('my child') address Antigone, and imply that the point of this narrative is that she too, however high-born, has not been exempt from deep unhappiness.

891–2 *born from ancient kings*: the Greek says she was 'born of the ancient race of the descendants of Erechtheus'—Erechtheus was the founder-king of Athens.

998 ff. *divination . . . all kinds of birds*: birds inhabit the space between humans and the gods, and so their behaviour provided a kind of divination. In the following lines (1005 ff.) the proper progress of burnt sacrifices, which fails here, is another sign.

1021–2 *Nor does the bird . . . of human blood*: these two lines are strangely worded and rather heavily tacked on. It is more than possible that one or both were later additions.

1037–8 *import electron coins*: Creon's rejection of Tiresias makes much of his belief that the prophet has been corrupted by money. Electron was an alloy of gold and silver found in some rivers in Asia Minor. The Lydians made coins from it.

1063–76 *This is to pay . . . these selfsame wrongs*: this crucial passage gives Tiresias' definitive account of how Creon has gone wrong—see also p. 9. He has interfered with the vertical ordering of the cosmos, and has distorted the functions of the gods of the dead. He has done this by keeping the dead above the surface of the earth (Polynices), and putting the living below it (Antigone). He will be punished through the same displacement, finding himself living on among dead bodies.

1077–9 *Now look and see . . . in your house*: rather like an allegory. Creon has accused Tiresias of being false like a coin of base metal, and made to look plausible by bribery, like silver-plating. The grief that is about to strike Creon's house will, on the contrary, be like rubbing the coin and finding that it is genuine all the way through.

1080–3 *And all the cities . . . the smoke from altars*: there were myths about the unburied bodies of the other commanders of the Seven who fought against Thebes; how they were eventually buried; and how their descendants were eventually avenged. But none of this is alluded to at all elsewhere in this play, so these lines seem intrusive. They are also rather ineptly worded, and I am inclined to agree with those editors who believe they have been added to the Sophocles. This will have been done by someone, probably an actor, who wanted to bring in an allusion to those other well-known—but irrelevant—stories.

1115–52 [*Sixth Choral Song*]: this song of two pairs of stanzas is entirely taken up by a prayer to Dionysus, pleading for him to come to Thebes, the city where he was born. (The technical term for this kind of prayer is 'kletic hymn'.) It is often claimed that it is jubilant in tone, as though the chorus mistakenly believes that the conflict has all been resolved, and that Dionysus is being summoned for celebration. It should be read, rather, as a plea, even slightly desperate, for help for the city in its troubles ('her people suffer with attacks of malign disease' 1140–1). It emphasizes Dionysus' joyful aspects only in the hope of potential celebration.

There are many features typical of this sort of hymn, some rather esoteric. The 'god of many names' is summoned by various cult-titles, notably Baccheus (1121) and Iacchos (1152). He is called from a range of places that he haunts: Italy (1119); Eleusis, the cult-centre of Demeter (1119–21); Delphi and the heights of Parnassus above (1126–30, 1144); Nysa (see 1131 below). The god is summoned with his special attendants and followers: the Nymphs of Parnassus (1129); callers of his cult-cry (1135); night-time cult-followers (1146–8); and maenads (1150–2).

1115–18 *son of Theban maid and thunderer Zeus*: Zeus impregnated the Theban princess, Semele, daughter of Cadmus, the legendary founder of Thebes; so Dionysus has special local connections. These are emphasized through allusions to the river Ismenus (1124); the story of the warriors sprung from dragon's teeth (1125); the streets of Thebes (1135); and the local cults of bacchant maenads (1122, 1134–60, 1150–2).

1118–19 *through Italy*: cults of Dionysus were strong in Italy, which here means the Greek cities in the south of present-day Italy.

1119–21 *hospitable Eleusis' holy shrine*: Eleusis, on the coast not far from Athens, was 'hospitable' because the initiation cult of Demeter and Persephone celebrated there was open to everyone regardless of native city, gender, or status. The cult title Iacchos (see also 1152) was associated with both Persephone and Dionysus.

1126–30 *double crests . . . Castalian stream*: Dionysus' association with Delphi is conveyed through geographical allusions: the 'double crests' are the

Phaedriades (the 'Shining Rocks'), two crags that tower above the shrine; the stream of Castalia flows down between them and has a fountain just below the shrine; the Corycian cave is not far distant above the Phaedriades on the slopes of Mount Parnassus.

1131 *Nysa*: location uncertain, but probably on the island of Euboea.

1139 *struck by the lightning bolt*: the story was that, under the influence of Hera's jealousy, Semele asked for Zeus to visit her in his true form: she was immolated by his lightning-bolt.

1150–2 *your maenads . . . your rite*: in the Greek the bacchant maenads are called 'Thyades', and they sing to 'lord Iacchos', a cult-title associated with Eleusis (see on 1119–21 above).

1180 *Eurydice*: there has been no previous mention of Creon's wife, and it may be that Sophocles invented this name for her. It was, however, implied at line 1164 that Creon had other children as well as Haemon.

1191 *I'm well experienced in grief*: Eurydice's allusion to past suffering is further explained later at 1302–4—see note.

1216–17 *go through . . . torn down*: the exact details are not clear (and the text may be faulty), but it seems that Antigone's cell was partly a natural cavern and partly man-made; and that she was sealed in by a wall that Haemon has broken through.

1245 [*SD*] *Eurydice goes indoors*: it is very unusual for a named character to go off in silence like this. But this departure of a noble woman to take her own life after hearing terrible news is, in fact, closely similar to the exit of Deianeira at *Deianeira* 812.

1257–end [*Lyric Dialogue*]: Creon returns from the scene of death described by the messenger to be met by further death at home. He has the body of Haemon with him—the text suggests he is carrying the corpse himself, at least at first. Much of the scene is sung in emotional lyric metres, interspersed with some spoken lines. Most of this lyric dialogue with the chorus consists of variations on the expression of his regret for his now fully acknowledged mistakes.

1293 [*SD*] *The body of Eurydice . . .*: it is likely that Eurydice's corpse was carried out by attendants: Creon then has both bodies close to him. This is one argument against supposing that the *ekkyklema* was employed; also there is not the usual indication of 'open the doors so that you can see . . .'—see further p. xxii.

1301–2 *Before the altar . . . sharpened point*: unfortunately there are textual problems in the first line, and then a line is missing from our manuscripts. The translation makes a guess at the sense. It is clear, however, that Eurydice stabbed herself at an altar, most likely that of 'household Zeus', dangerously dismissed by Creon back at line 487.

1303 *the glorious fate of Megareus*: this alludes to stories that one of Creon's sons had to give up his life in order to save his father and to ensure the victory of Thebes in the battle. A version of this is dramatized in Euripides' *Phoenician Women*, where he is called Menoeceus. The transmitted text says 'glorious bed', which some editors emend to 'empty bed', and others, more plausibly, to 'glorious fate'.

1334–end *That is the future . . .* : Creon is now totally without power, and has to submit to others. The chorus speak of 'those who should take care of matters'. This might imply that others now rule the city; but refers primarily to the gods.

DEIANEIRA

7–9 *Pleuron . . . the Achelous*: Deianeira grew up in Aetolia, the south-western part of mainland Greece, to the north of the mouth of the Gulf of Corinth. Her father Oineus was king of Pleuron, and her brother was another important mythological figure, Meleager.

10–14 *in triple form . . . his shaggy beard*: the physiology of these three forms is not precise. In art Achelous is often shown with an anthropomorphic body but a bull's head, or else like a Centaur. The third form here seems to suggest a bull's body with the implication of taurine genitals. Small wonder Deianeira is so horrified! And is this 'bed' of his (17) a river bed?

19 *son of Zeus and Alcmene*: Zeus famously took on the form of Amphitryon, king of Thebes, in order to go to bed with his wife Alcmene. She went on to bear non-identical twins, the semi-divine Heracles and the purely human Iolaus.

35 *at somebody's command*: Deianeira prefers not to name Eurystheus, king of Argos, who has commanded Heracles' labours.

38 *Iphitus*: at this stage nothing is explained about Iphitus beyond the fact that Heracles killed him. This will turn out, however, to have been an important event, more fully narrated later in the play, especially by the herald Lichas at lines 269 ff.

39 *here displaced in Trachis*: it will emerge later that the family of Heracles had been settled at Tiryns, near Argos. It is never explained in this play why it was Trachis that they moved to—see p. 67 and map. Elsewhere it was said that Ceyx, king of Trachis, was a family friend.

44–7 *fifteen months . . . written tablet*: again the significance of unexplained details in Deianeira's prologue—the precise time and the written tablet—will become clear later in the play.

54 *a clutch of sons*: Hyllus is the only son of Heracles and Deianeira who is named and who appears in this play. He will be important in the final scene.

69–70 *a Lydian lady*: it was a well-known story that Heracles was sold to Omphale, queen of Lydia, to be her slave for a year.

74 *Eurytus' city in Euboea*: Heracles' sack of Eurytus' city of Oechalia was already celebrated in epic. Sophocles locates this somewhere on the large island of Euboea (see map).

79–81 *That either . . . days at peace*: the real meaning of this oracle will only emerge later in the play—see pp. 74–5.

84 *or else . . . father's death*: all editors are agreed that this line is an intrusion—perhaps originally an explanation written in the margin.

94–102 [*First Choral Song*]: the first stanza calls on Sun, who sees all, to tell where Heracles is. It opens with a kind of high-style riddle.

100–1 *Could he be . . . Black Sea strait*: the interpretation of this pair of alternatives is far from sure. This version takes the word *pontios*, which could mean 'of the sea', to refer to the Pontos, the Black Sea; and it takes the 'twin continents' to refer to the 'Pillars of Heracles', the ancient name for the Straits of Gibraltar. The pair of references then stand for east and west.

112–21 *As on the open sea* . . . : there are difficulties in the interpretation of this stanza, and the likely reference to waves dipping and lifting Heracles' fortunes requires a textual emendation. Two elaborations in the Greek have been simplified: the original has a 'Cretan sea', which was notorious for rough weather, and grandly calls Heracles 'the descendant of Cadmus' (founder of Thebes, home of Alcmene).

171–2 *ancient oak-tree* . . . *pair of Doves*: the venerable sanctuary of Zeus at Dodona in remote north-western Greece was known for its oak trees, which some say spoke the oracles. This one here is delivered by the 'pair of doves', but it is disputed whether this means actual birds, or was, as preferred here, the title of priestesses. There is more on this mysterious site at 1166 ff., on which see note.

178 [*SD*] *The old man approaches* . . . : the old man is given no identity beyond being local, and familiar with both Deianeira and Lichas. Those who bring good news tend to hope for some reward.

183 *choicest offerings* . . . : it was pious custom after any triumph to offer 'first fruits' to the gods. This will prove important in the story.

188–9 *herald Lichas* . . . *Oxen Mead*: Lichas already figured in the Heracles story before Sophocles. The role of *keryx*, herald, was significant as a kind of ceremonial attendant and diplomat. It is unknown whether 'the meadow where oxen graze' was a specific known locality; but in giving it a capital letter I have supposed that it was.

194 *folk of Malis*: Malis was the area between the sea and Trachis (see map).

200 *Oeta's uncropped meadow-grass*: the first allusion in the play to this significant mountain, the most prominent in this area (see map). There were often high meadows regarded as sacred and left uncropped.

205–24 [*Choral Song*]: this is an unusual occurrence in Greek tragedy: a stanza of song arising directly out of the action and not standing as an ode between two episodes. The last lines (221–4) actually introduce the following scene. The song takes the form of a celebratory hymn of thanks to Apollo and Artemis, leading into a maenadic invocation of Dionysus. (There are several places where the text is problematic.)

205 *halloo*: the *ololygmos* was a ritual cry of jubilation, often associated with women.

217–20 *aulos* . . . *ivy*: the *aulos* was a double-pipe with two separate reeds which made a piercing sound. It was the instrument that accompanied tragic lyric, and was associated, although not exclusively, with Dionysus. Ivy was particular to his cult.

237–8 *There is a headland* . . . *Zeus of Caeneum*: at the northern end of Euboea there is a substantial westward promontory which projects into the Gulf of Malis (see map). The mountain on this, some 740 m. high, was called

Cenaeum (Greek *Kenaion*). The tip of this cape is only a short way from Malis and Trachis. This would be familiar to anyone who had journeyed to this part of Greece by sea.

241 *these women* . . . : Lichas unobtrusively introduces the fact that the women are slaves captured from Oechalia. He is being discreet.

252–3 *He was sold . . . he himself admits*: these two lines rather clumsily expand on what has been said already; they may well have been added by an actor.

257 *child*: this singular is usually taken to mean (plural) children. But it seems more likely that Lichas is portrayed as making a slip, in view of the fact that it is a particular child of Eurytus that Heracles was most interested in, as will emerge eventually.

260–1 *he alone . . . for this disgrace*: there are signs that Lichas' account is 'economical with the truth', but they are not blatant. It is claimed, for example, that Eurytus was entirely to blame for his own downfall, but it soon emerges that the issue was not so simple.

265 *arrows*: a passing allusion to Heracles' superhuman bow whose arrows never missed the mark.

270 *Iphytus*: evidently the basic story was already so well known that there is no need to explain that Iphytus was the son of Eurytus.

277 *by trickery*: it is implied that Heracles had climbed with Iphitus to the high viewing-point, and had then pushed him off while he was occupied with staring into the distance.

305 *or if . . . me alive*: this line weakens the thought. Either Sophocles 'nodded' or it was added.

309 *in all these things*: it will transpire that Iole has experienced sex, though not motherhood.

313 *she alone* . . . : it is hard to know whether her difference was conveyed in stage actuality, and, if so, how. Much easier to convey in a small modern theatre!

335 [*SD*] *Lichas and the slave women* . . . : this is a significant turning point. The old man makes Deianeira turn back from Lichas' deceit and from her ignorance to face the truth.

354 *Eros*: while usually translated as 'love', Eros is more specifically sexual desire. It is often personified as a winged boy-child of Aphrodite.

362–4 *claiming that . . . her father*: there are problems in the wording of the Greek here and most editors cut out two lines, but this translation offers a possible interpretation.

368 *if he's molten with desire*: the old man's account has been leading up to this unusually intense wording.

402 ff. [*SD*] *The old man intervenes*: throughout the following dialogue the old man's tone is bluff and combative.

444 *and over me . . . like me*: assuming that this line is by Sophocles (some editors have had doubts), Deianeira surely cannot be saying, as might seem at first sight, that she and Iole have themselves experienced overwhelming sexual desire: it is the overwhelming desire of Heracles that has controlled their lives.

459 *What is so terrible in knowing?*: the play supplies a bitter answer to this apparently harmless question. See further p. 74.

460 ff. *Heracles has been to bed . . .* : the common knowledge, as it seems, that Heracles has dallied with many women previously is only introduced here. Deianeira's tolerance of this seems plausible at this stage. The Greek in lines 462–3 ('not even if utterly consumed . . .') might refer to either Heracles or Iole, but she is surely talking about him not her.

496 *splendid retinue*: there is a touch of bitterness in this description of the slave women including Iole. The 'gifts . . . in return for gifts' will turn out to be unexpected.

503 *this bridal-bed*: it is no surprise, after the previous scene, that this choral song is about the power of Aphrodite (called, as often, 'Cypris'), but when it turns from gods to mortals, it is not the recent battle for Iole that is the subject: 'this bridal-bed' goes back to the contest for Deianeira between Heracles and the river Achelous, as recalled in the prologue. The word translated as 'bridal bed', *akoitis*, can mean simply wife, but it incorporates a word for 'bed', which is relevant here.

510–11 *Oiniadai . . . bacchic Thebes*: Oiniadai was a city in Aetolia near the mouth of the river Achelous. Thebes, the birthplace of Heracles, was also the birthplace of Dionysus, and often associated with his bacchant followers.

554 *the plan*: this translates a plausible emendation of the text which says (in Greek) 'pain'.

555 ff. *I have a present given . . .* : this is the first we have heard about Nessus, but he has features reminiscent of Achelous. He is an old-style creature, a 'shaggy-breasted' Centaur, though it is not specified whether he has two legs or four. The river Euinos is the first river that Heracles and the newly won Deianeira will have come to as they journeyed eastwards from Pleuron.

564 *upon his shoulders*: it is not clear whether this means his human-shape shoulders or on his horse-shape upper back. Either way his hands are free to assault her sexually.

572–4 *Collect the clots . . . Hydra's fangs*: it is taken as known that Heracles' invincible arrows were tipped with venom from the Hydra. This monster with multiple snake-heads lived at Lerna, near Argos, and Heracles killed it as one of his labours.

580 *this garment*: Deianeira must make it clear that the impregnated garment is inside the casket she is holding.

630–2 *What more . . . from that side*: it is difficult to tell what these lines are meant to convey. Deianeira shows awareness that she has not given Lichas any expression of personal affection to convey to Heracles; yet the lines seem to be said to herself more than to him.

633–9 *All you who live . . . Hot Springs*: the first stanza of this outwardly celebratory ode consists entirely of a call to all the people around Trachis, all the way from the coast, where Heracles will land, through the coastal plain of Malis, to Mount Oeta that dominates the region. The harbours of this part of Greece were held to be protected by Artemis (here identified in the Greek as 'the virgin of the golden arrows'). The most famous landmark was the narrow pass between mountain and sea (now silted up), where there are hot sulphur springs, and which was known as Thermopylae, meaning, literally, 'Hot-water Gateway'. There was a sanctuary of Demeter here, and it was the meeting place for an alliance of all the towns of this part of central Greece. It was also the site of the famous stand by Spartan soldiers against the Persian invasion in 480.

653 *Ares frenzied*: the wording carries an echo of Heracles' undertaking a whole war because he was driven wild with passion.

658 *From Euboea*: the Greek says literally 'After leaving the altar on the island . . .'.

661–2 *let him come . . . arouses his desire*: while it is clear that it is concerned with Heracles' being made to desire Deianeira, the Greek text is very uncertain here. Among several other choices, this translation accepts an emendation from 'of the creature' (*theros*) to 'of the robe' (*pharous*).

696 *the sheep's wool . . . flaming glare*: this line seems clumsily worded and I am inclined to agree with editors who think that an actor added it to pad out the dramatic passage.

715 *Cheiron*: although he was known as a 'Centaur', Cheiron was of a different breed from the monster Centaurs, such as Nessus, and was both wise and immortal. There were various stories of how he came to be accidentally wounded by Heracles' arrow, and how Zeus allowed him to die.

752–3 *Cenaeum*: the extreme point of Euboea, closest to Malis—see note on 237–8. Lichas arrived from there, and has returned while Heracles has been preparing the precinct.

768–9 *like drapery . . . sculptor's hand*: the interpretation of this is disputed; but as the sculptors of this period developed highly sophisticated techniques for carving the appearance of fine drapery over human limbs, this makes for a vivid simile.

780 *a rock that stuck up from the sea*: some small islands off the cape were known—and still are known—as the Lichades, the Lichas Islands.

788 *Locris*: the mountainous mainland to the south.

809 *Erinys*: the plural Erinyes (often translated as 'Furies') were fearsome spirits of revenge. The singular here stands for their powers.

after 812 [*SD*] *Deianeira turns* . . . : on this departure in silence see the note on *Antigone* line 1245.

821–61 [*Fourth Choral Song*]: this choral ode is relatively closely tied to the dramatic context. In the first two stanzas the chorus dwells on the realization that the prophecy about Heracles reaching the end of his labours meant that he would then die. In the second pair they explore how Deianeira's response to Heracles' passion for Iole has led to his agony trapped in the robe of Nessus. The god behind all this is Cypris (Aphrodite).

825 *twelve years*: this is not consistent with the prophecy reported by Deianeira in the prologue, which spoke of fifteen months. But, given Heracles' labours, a prophecy specifying twelve years is no problem.

831–40 *So if compulsion* . . . : this stanza is enigmatically expressed, and there are some textual uncertainties. This translation adopts emendations for 'brewed with' and 'cloak'.

863–95 *Unless I'm wrong* . . . : there are some lyric patches in this dialogue between the chorus and the old serving woman. The distribution of lines between them is not certain, but editors mostly agree that the sung passages belong to the chorus, quite possibly split up among individual members.

893–5 *Just born . . . a mighty curse*: a powerful, rather macabre image, which suggests that, when Iole was admitted into the house, she was already pregnant, not with a human child but with an 'Erinys', translated here as 'curse'. On Erinys see note on 809.

903 *then she . . . from sight*: it is hard to see what this line means here, because immediately afterwards the old woman sees her, not hiding, but going around the house. It seems to be a misplaced doubling of line 914 where the old woman spies from a hiding place.

971 ff. *O my father* . . . : with technique that is unusual for Greek tragedy, Hyllus comes out from the palace exactly as the procession bringing Heracles arrives. Perhaps he should be thought of as having been looking out for them. And who is the old attendant in charge of the procession? He is never identified, but seems to have the role of a kind of medical supervisor. After the opening dialogue he fades out. This dialogue as far as line 1003 is in the chanted anapaestic metre.

1004–43 *Let me be* . . . : Heracles' agony now raises pitch, expressed in a pair of lyric stanzas. Both include five lines of dactylic hexameters, and there is a hexameter dialogue between the old man and Hyllus in between the stanzas. It is not easy to see what is the effect of this unusual recourse to the traditional metre of epic. Perhaps it evokes his ancient stature as a hero of epic poetry, now brought low?

1031 *Athena*: often portrayed as Heracles' protecting deity, although not elsewhere in this play.

1049–50 *Zeus' wife, nor loathed Eurystheus*: Hera, alluded to only here in the play, persecuted Heracles out of jealousy, and put him under the power of Eurystheus, named only here, who imposed the famous labours on him.

1058–9 *the Giants*: the *Gigantes* were huge offspring of Earth who challenged the Olympian gods. Heracles fought along with the Olympians when they won a celebrated primeval victory.

1091–1100 *It was with these . . . reaches of the world*: Heracles' labours were later classified as a set of twelve; but here he cites six, and speaks of 'innumerable' others. First in his list is the lion that marauded through the district of Nemea in the north-eastern Peloponnese, which was the most famous of all; its skin became an essential feature of the image of Heracles. The hydra at Lerna (see on lines 572–4) was not far distant from Nemea. He then includes a skirmish with the Centaurs, perhaps reminding the audience of Nessus. The Boar of Erymanthus was another marauding beast in the central Peloponnese. Finally he includes two more far-ranging and fantastical labours: fetching up Cerberus, the triple-headed hound that guarded the gate of Hades, and subduing the dragon that kept watch over the golden apples that grew in the land of the Hesperides in the far west (somewhere unspecific in the Atlantic).

1141 *Nessus the Centaur* . . . : Heracles scorns Trachis as too minor a place for anyone who could produce such a potion. But the name of Nessus changes the whole picture for him.

1151–4 *Your mother . . . within the town*: it is a consequence of Heracles' eventful and unstable life that his kin are scattered in different places from his past. It may be implied that his sons at Tiryns and Thebes are from other mothers, and that only those borne by Deianeira are in Trachis.

1166–8 *I visited . . . of many voices*: the strange and remote oracle of Zeus with its oak trees at Dodona has already been evoked at lines 171–2 (see note). The Selloi were the priests there, famous for sleeping on the ground and for keeping their feet unwashed.

1174 *these things are clearly falling into place*: Ezra Pound in his version (1954) adds a footnote to this line, 'This is the key phrase, for which the play exists . . .'. His text uses capitals:

'SPLENDOUR,
IT ALL COHERES.'

1191 *Mount Oeta*: the local mountain to the west of Trachis now becomes a more specific location. The site of the pyre, as established by archaeology, is not actually at the highest point of the mountain, and it is disputed whether Sophocles' original text specified this.

1211 *you cannot face*: the common story was that it was Heracles' friend Philoctetes who lit the pyre, and that Heracles gave him his bow as reward. This is an important motif in Sophocles' *Philoctetes*.

1224–6 *do not let . . . pressed to mine*: the argument that his son and no one else should have sex with this woman because he has done so himself is hardly cogent—and it seems grotesque to call the issue 'small' (1217, 1229). Hyllus himself is understandably repelled by the idea. At the same time there may be some sense of a higher will setting up this dynastic marriage, which was well known in myth.

1259–end: the metre changes to anapaests for the final movements of the play.

1264–72 *Grant to me . . . shows them as shameful*: this condemnation of the gods for their lack of feeling and sense of obligation is remarkably vehement and direct. The contrast between gods and humans is brought out by strikingly paired wordings. Hyllus asks to be given great *syn-gnomosyne,* 'with-understandingness', a special coinage related to the Greek for 'forgiveness': this is contrasted with the gods who display *a-gnomosyne*, 'non-understandingness'. Furthermore this condemnation is, in its context, not obviously mistaken or unjustified. Hyllus acknowledges that humans cannot know how the future may change things, but he is surely right that their present human suffering seems to show indifference from the gods.

1275–9 *You as well . . . is not Zeus*: these lines are seriously problematic, so much so that there must be doubt whether we have the ending of the play as composed by Sophocles. The closing lines of Greek tragedy are nearly always delivered by the chorus, and the final line here 'Nothing of all this is not Zeus' seems characteristically choral. The words are not at all fitted to Hyllus, both because they do not follow in sequence from his previous lines, and especially because the final sentiment is deeply discordant with his condemnation of the gods.

The most obvious problem is that the lines are addressed to a 'young woman'—the word *parthenos* used here usually implies 'virgin', but signifies more precisely 'unmarried young woman'. If these lines were spoken by the chorus or chorus-leader addressing themselves, this should be a plural not a singular—and elsewhere they are usually called *gynaikes*, 'women'. The most appropriate person for '*parthenos*' to refer to should be Iole (who has been recently identified as 'the *parthenos* of Eurytus' at 1219). But there is no indication whatsoever that she has been brought back on stage at any point; and these lines seem too abrupt and perfunctory to suffice for summoning her outside. Also it does not seem at all appropriate for the chorus to summon her. There might be a dramatic case in favour of her being called on to participate in Heracles' funeral procession, but these lines do not seem enough to justify such a significant and disturbing move. It has been objected against identifying her as the *parthenos* that she has not witnessed 'recent dreadful killings', but she has—in her home town of Oechalia. So it remains far from clear both who delivers these final lines (but not Hyllus, I believe), and whom they are addressed to.

after 1279 [*SD*] *All accompany . . .* : the procession sets off for the mountain, site of the celebrated pyre of Heracles. This would probably have put the audience in mind of the stories of his being taken up from the pyre to a blessed immortality on Olympus. This is not, however, at all explicit or assured within the play, which ends on a grim rather than a redemptive note. See further pp. 73–6.

ELECTRA

1 *he who was . . . host at Troy*: there is good evidence in ancient sources that this grandiloquent flourish, which is the first line in the Greek, was added by later actors.

2–8 *here you see . . . shrine of Hera*: the play opens with Orestes being shown a panorama of the ancestral kingdom from which he has been exiled. The setting is Mycene, the Homeric palace, rather than the city of Argos, which makes this scene geographically plausible. Mycene is set on a prominent foothill some 10 km north of Argos with an expansive view over the plain below. The river Inachus (line 5), which flows through the plain, is associated with the story of the river-god's daughter Io, who was impregnated by Zeus. It is questionable whether the temple of Apollo in the city (lines 6–7) would have been visible from that distance, but the most important and conspicuous religious site in the whole area, the great temple of Hera (line 7–8), was less than 3 km away to the south-east (so 'to the left').

10 *rich in blood*: a grim word-play of *polyphthoron* with *polychrysous*, 'rich in gold', the Homeric epithet in the previous line.

16 *Pylades*: the son of Strophius of Phocis who gave shelter to Orestes during his exile. They are nearly always together as a pair in tragedy.

23 *Most cherished of all servants*: the old man is an especially responsible slave with the role of *paidagogos*, which means, in effect, carer of male children (often rather anachronistically translated as 'tutor'). He is far from servile, and behaves as a respected participant throughout the play.

45 *Phanoteus*: another ruler in Phocis, but on bad terms with Pylades' father Strophius.

47 *swearing it on oath*: this would seem to be a dangerous exploitation of the gods (and is never actually done in the scene). So it may support a 'contaminated' interpretation of Orestes' ethics—see p. 132. For those who believe this is inconsistent with the general portrayal of Orestes, a slight change in the Greek (from *horkon* to *ogkon*) would produce the meaning 'giving it full weight'.

49 *Pythian Games*: these contests were held every fourth year at Delphi in honour of Apollo, who was given the cult-title Pythios.

61 *No spoken word . . . brings gain*: this rather cynical attitude is not in keeping. Possibly the line was added later as being on the same kind of subject.

62–4 *often heard the stories*: this would probably prompt people to think of Odysseus in the *Odyssey*.

86–120 *Limpid sunlight . . .*: Electra's opening lament and call for vengeance is in a type of anapaestic metre which was probably chanted rather than sung. Its language is, however, in quite a 'high' lyric-style register.

87 *share in dawn*: this is an attractive emendation of the transmitted text which says that the light and air have a share of 'earth'.

107–8 *like the nightingale*: Procne killed her son Itys in order to punish her rapist husband. She was metamorphosed into the nightingale, and her song, with its repeated call of 'Itys, Itys', was regarded as the archetypal lament.

110–12 *O you house . . . Erinyes*: Electra summons a whole series of non-Olympian gods of the underworld before she enunciates her prayer for revenge. These are gods so dark and frightening that they are often left unnamed, especially the Erinyes, yet Electra names them without any reserve. The Erinyes are often translated as 'Furies' (*Furiae* in Latin), but that does not do justice to their uncanny horror.

121–250 [*First Choral Song*]: instead of the usual purely choral entrance-song, this long lyric takes the form of three pairs of stanzas followed by an 'epode', each shared between the chorus and Electra, and giving her the conclusion.

148 *mourns for Itys, Itys*: this is the mourning nightingale again (see note on 107–8 above). The Greek adds 'messenger of Zeus', but this has been omitted as its significance is obscure.

150–2 *Niobe*: Niobe was another archetype of grief. When all her children had been killed by the gods, she mourned until she was eventually turned to a rock with water trickling down it (see also on *Antigone* 823–33).

156–7 *sisters quiet within*: the chorus say that Electra has other more passive sisters indoors, and they name Chrysothemis, who will play a part later in the play, and Iphianassa (omitted from the translation).

163 *Orestes*: Electra alluded to her brother at line 117, but this is the first time after the prologue that he is actually named, with the chorus holding his name back until the last word of their stanza.

180–1 *Crisa's meadow*: Crisa is in the plain beneath Delphi, and so in the same area of Greece as Phocis.

193 ff. *Pitiful scream when* . . . : the change of tone and sudden passion here is so vivid that it seems strange that it is the previously restrained chorus who deliver these lines. It is tempting to wonder whether they might have been delivered by Electra herself, but in that case the normal stanza-pairing would be seriously disrupted.

271 ff. *And see the crowning act* . . . : Electra, who sleeps alone and remains unmarried, particularly resents and is disgusted by the sex between her mother and her usurping partner, Aegisthus.

278 ff. *On the contrary* . . . : a travesty of any kind of memorial event for the dead.

380–2 *they are going to . . . excavated cell*: this is reminiscent of the punishment that Creon imposes on Antigone.

417–23 *It's said that in her dream . . . the country of Mycene*: it has been disputed whether this means that in the dream they had sex, but there would be little significance in their merely being together. If, however, the overshadowing tree grows after they have had sex, then that is a potent reminder for Clytemnestra that the pair of them are Orestes' parents.

428–30: *And so I beg you . . . in trouble*: there is no convincing way of making these three lines fit here, where they merely break the sequence between the dream and Electra's reaction to it. They reflect the previous argument between the two sisters, and are either displaced from there, or somehow added by a later editor in the wrong place here from another context.

442–6 *at whose hands . . . his own hair*: the mutilation of the corpse and wiping off blood on the murdered man's hair are both rather primitive rituals that attempt to counteract the power of vengeance.

489–91 *With many feet . . . Erinys*: the Erinyes (see on 110–12 above) are not envisaged with a recognized form, although they are often portrayed with snakes. The picture here builds up the sense of menace.

494–5 *unbed, unmarriage*: this translation tries to reflect the unusual wording of the Greek, which does not mean that there was literally no bed or no marriage, but that they were somehow perverted or negated. The word for 'unbed' is *alektra*, which is close to Electra's own name—the significance of this is, however, enigmatic.

503–15 *Calamitous was that horse-race . . .* : after the pair of stanzas arising out of Clytemnestra's dream, and looking forward to the punishment of the ruling pair, this single stanza (known as an 'epode') suddenly turns to the distant past. It digs up a guilt-ridden episode about Pelops at the beginning of the dynastic family-tree, and thus raises the question of whether the family has some kind of inherited corruption. King Oenomaus challenged and defeated all suitors in a chariot-race for the hand of his daughter Hippodameia. Pelops (who came from Asia Minor) got the charioteer Myrtilus to tamper with Oenomaus' vehicle so that it fatally crashed. But as his 'reward' Pelops threw him to his death in the sea. The same word *polyponos*, translated as 'calamitous', comes at the beginning with 'this land' and at the end with 'this house'.

530 ff. *he was the one . . .* : Clytemnestra recalls how her daughter Iphigeneia was sacrificed by her father Agamemnon at Aulis to ensure the fleet's departure for Troy; so she claims justified revenge as her motivation for killing her husband.

532–3 *it was not pain he felt*: an unusually explicit allusion, for Greek tragedy, to the physical pleasure of sex. This bitter jibe is in keeping with the lively rhetoric of Clytemnestra's defence.

563 ff. *And then ask Artemis . . .* : there were various accounts of why Artemis held up the Greek fleet at Aulis leading to the sacrifice of Iphigeneia. Electra's version here is not greatly to the credit of Agamemnon—see also next note.

573–4 *there was no other way . . . nor on to Troy*: it is not true that the army could not disperse back overland to their homes in Greece, unlike the way that they could not set sail for Troy. Electra's claim that Agamemnon was 'forced' to sacrifice Iphigeneia is special pleading.

610–11 *I see you . . . on her side*: it is not clear who says these lines and about whom. The interpretation here is uncertain.

637–42 *Please listen . . .* : the implication seems to be that Clytemnestra is secretly praying for the death of her own son, Orestes.

659 *for Zeus' children . . . everything*: this rather pedantic line weakens Clytemnestra's concluding words, and may well be an addition.

668 *I welcome the good omen*: it seems as though the old servant has arrived in answer to Clytemnestra's prayer. And if his message were true, then it would be just as she secretly wished: in fact the truth is the opposite.

691 *for running . . . as established*: this line, which does not even seem to scan in Greek, is clearly a pedagogic note that has somehow got into the text.

693 *naming him*: it was an important element in Greek athletic contests that the victor's name was announced along with his father's name and his home-city, reflecting glory on them as well. This touch, which would not be welcome in Clytemnestra's ears, is part of what makes the whole speech so plausible.

698 ff. *When on the final day . . .* : the most prestigious event of all was the four-horse chariot race. This was held in the flat plain of Crisa (see 180–1) below Delphi.

701 ff. *One was . . .* : this 'sports-commentary' kind of detail serves both to authenticate the account, and to build up the suspense for what we have been warned (at 696–7) will end disastrously for Orestes. 'Libya' here means from a Greek city in Libya; the most famous was Cyrene.

after 719 *And up till now . . .* : at this point in the transmitted Greek text there are three lines that clearly belong to a later stage in the race. Assuming that they originally came from this narrative, the place where they seem to fit best is twenty lines later after line 740. This is where they have been placed in this translation ('And as he went around . . . holding in the left'). We cannot know how they came to be displaced.

727 *Barce*: this was a Greek city in Libya. The course was two parallel 'lanes' with turning posts at either end. It seems that the swerve here was so bad that it went across into the course for the other direction (a bit like swerving across the central reservation of a dual-carriageway).

743 *tightened up*: the transmitted Greek says 'loosened', but a slight emendation produces this much better sense.

746–7 *wrapped round himself*: it was part of the highly skilled technique of charioteers that they would wind the reins round their bodies and arms so that they could control them more subtly. This makes a crash far more dangerous (the same detail occurs in the account of Hippolytus' fatal crash in Euripides' tragedy).

755–6 *most dear to him*: it will be especially painful for Electra to hear of Orestes so mangled that his closest kin would not recognize him.

792 *Nemesis*: a powerful moral force, regarded as a deity, Nemesis is the sense of indignation provoked by outrageous behaviour, especially behaviour that shows no sense of shame. It is not (as popularly used now in English) the punishment itself, but the indignation that leads towards the desire to punish.

816 *my father's . . . well with me*: this line is intrusive, probably the work of an actor padding out the role.

823 ff. *Lyric dialogue lament . . .* : it is already three hundred lines since the last choral song, and one might be expected here in between two scenes. The emotions of Electra are, however, so strong and central that Sophocles composes a lyric dialogue between her and the chorus rather than have her fall silent.

837–48 *Amphiaraus' story . . .* : the chorus try to comfort Electra by recalling a myth that parallels her situation in that it is about a woman who treacherously killed her husband; yet he remained powerful nonetheless after death, and their son eventually avenged his father by killing his mother. Amphiaraus' wife Eriphyle was bribed with a golden necklace to send her husband to his death in battle; she was killed in due course by their son Alcmaeon. The difference, as Electra is quick to point out, is that Orestes, unlike Alcmaeon, is dead—or so she believes.

920 ff. *How I've been pitying . . .* : it is an indication of Electra's dominating character that Chrysothemis gives way to her so easily—although, in fact, she is right and Electra wrong.

1007–8 *It is not death . . . make it sure*: editors are agreed that the point made in these two lines does not fit here, and that they do not belong in Sophocles' text.

1050–4 *Well I am going . . . foolishness*: many editors think that these lines have been added to the original, but their reasons for this are not very strong. They object that Electra's saying 'I'll never ever follow you' is vacuous, but, in fact, it is strongly in keeping with the vow that she made at lines 817 ff. that she would stay outside and never again go into the palace—see also p. 131.

1058 ff. [*Third Choral Song*]: up until this point the chorus has always advised caution and moderation, but now they express whole-hearted and vivid support for Electra's stand.

1064 *Themis*: a divine power, often associated with Zeus, who is believed to ensure that obligations are ultimately maintained in proper order.

1080 *demon pair*: the Greek says 'the double Erinys', i.e. the pair of Erinyes, Clytemnestra and Aegisthus—on the Erinyes see note on 110–12 above.

before 1098 [*SD*] *Orestes and Pylades enter . . .* : the audience will have noticed the small bronze urn, supposedly containing the ashes of Orestes, before it is first alluded to at 1113. The old servant prepared for its importance both in the prologue (54–6) and in his report of Orestes' death (757–60).

1170 *for I see . . . no pain*: this banal line detracts from the strong ending of Electra's lament. It is typical of an actor wanting to stretch out the part.

1177 *famous*: famous because she is a princess? Or because of her inconsolable and vengeful grief for her father?

1220–6. *What are you saying . . . keep this hold of me*: with the intense emotion many of these lines are split between the pair.

1232–87 During this scene Electra mostly sings in emotional lyrics while Orestes speaks calmly, trying to restrain her loud jubilation. There are textual problems in the Greek throughout, especially in the closing lines. A couple of very brief interchanges have been omitted.

1315–17 *You've had a strange effect . . .* : this peculiar notion seems to be the product of Electra's obsession with her dead father. She also greets the old servant as her 'father': at line 1361.

1322–5 *I think you should . . .* : editors disagree over who says these lines. The first line and a half ('I think . . . coming from the house') might be the chorus or (less likely) Orestes, but it makes far the best sense for the other two and half lines ('Please enter, strangers . . . distress them to receive it') to be spoken by Electra, behaving, in case the person entering is hostile, as though she had only had impersonal contact with the strangers.

1385 *Ares*: the god representing aggressive action.

1388 *unrelenting hounds*: this image may well evoke the Erinyes who were characterized as hunting dogs in Aeschylus' *Oresteia*.

1395–7 *Hermes*: Hermes is often associated with trickery and stealth.

1406 *somebody*: Electra knows perfectly well whose cry this is, and her cold use of 'somebody' here and again in 1410 verges on vindictive inhumanity. The chorus' disturbed response is more 'normal'.

1414 *strike twice as hard*: this is usually taken to mean 'strike a second time', but the emphasis indicates 'double strength'.

1417 *The curses now begin their work*: on this line, coming after 1413–14, see the introduction, pp. 133–4.

around 1428–30 *<three or four brief lines missing . . .>*: it is likely that the two sections which include lyric dialogue (i.e. 1398–1421 and 1422–41) were metrically matching, and in that case some short lines are missing from around here. Editors are not agreed on exactly how they were arranged. We might, however, have expected 'Stop now, because I can see clear | that there's Aegisthus coming into view' to have been delivered by Electra rather than the chorus, were it not for the metrical matching of stanzas.

1455 *a most unenviable sight*: Sophocles unobtrusively prepares for the supposed death of Orestes to be demonstrated by his actual body, and not by his ashes in an urn. This coup has been plotted without being made explicit in the dialogue.

after 1463 [*SD*] *Electra opens the stage-doors*: this is a classic use of the stage machinery of the *ekkyklema* (see p. xxii). The doors are opened and a tableau is rolled out on a platform; this is taken to make the interior scene visible to the outside world (including the audience). Here, indeed, Aegisthus calls on the local public to view the corpse.

1466–7 *O Zeus . . . I cannot say*: Aegisthus puts on a high-minded act for public consumption. Orestes' fate, he says, means that he must have incurred some sort of divine envy or resentment (the Greek word is *phthonos*). But then he 'modestly' adds that it is not for him to judge whether that meant divine condemnation (the word here is *nemesis*, see on line 792 above). He then goes on to say that it is appropriate for him to display some grief at the death of kin (his cousin)—although it is clear that he is really gloating. His moralizings are ironically applicable to Clytemnestra and himself.

1475 *Who don't you recognize?*: he recognizes the corpse of Clytemnestra, of course, but has not quite yet identified Orestes.

1485–6 *When people . . . further time*: these two lines are not in the main text of our oldest and best manuscript, but are added in the margin. A possible explanation of this is that it was disputed in antiquity whether or not they belonged in Sophocles' text. They do not really fit this context and pointlessly hold up Electra's urgency.

1487–90 *convey him . . . his past of wrongs*: although this has been disputed, it seems clear enough that what Electra means by this is that his body should be left exposed as carrion for the dogs and birds. This is a standard 'heroic' humiliation for hated enemies, and nothing less will suit Electra's words. While her demand may not be ethically admirable, this is not the same as the situation in *Antigone* and *Aias*, where a figure in authority actively forbids burial by anyone on pain of death. These unreservedly vindictive words are the last spoken by Electra in the play—see also p. 130.

1497–8 *Is it inevitable . . . and those to come?*: on the important and contested question whether this implied threat and other insinuations made by Aegisthus here are empty or have power, see the introduction pp. 134–5. It is telling that the only two other times the name of Pelops has cropped up in the play are in the introduction to 'this, the palace of the dynasty of Pelops, rich in blood' in line 10, and in the chorus' evocation of his guilt in the story of Myrtilus at 502–15 (see note there). (The meaning 'all the horrors' involves a small emendation from the Greek, which takes 'all/wholly' with 'inevitable'—a less good sequence.)

1505–7 *This punishment . . . would not be rife*: this moralizing proclamation, advocating widespread capital punishment, is inevitably caught up in the crucial interpretative issue of the extent to which the play does or does not encourage unqualified approval of Electra and Orestes. On this see pp. 131–4 in the introduction. These three lines set up this particular case of Aegisthus as an example of the universal rule that crime should be summarily punished by death. There are, however, phrases here which are so banal and crude that they do no justice to the subtlety of Sophocles' play.

Thus, Aegisthus is not simply an example of 'those who want to act outside the laws'; nor does his death set a deterrent to all those who are guilty of 'criminality'. This is a highly charged dramatic situation, and given Orestes' bitterness and his eagerness to get on with killing Aegisthus, this little sermon on how to purge the world of all villainy is, I believe, an inept intrusion.

1508–10 *So, you dynasty . . . present action*: these few closing anapaests from the chorus have also been condemned as inauthentic by some editors. But, unlike with the previous lines, there is nothing objectionable in their content; indeed they are typical of the rather pedestrian choral lines that mark the transition from play to applause, and the quasi-metatheatrical allusion to the action reaching its conclusion is typical. The editorial objections to these lines have been primarily linguistic; and, while it is true that there are some features here that are not standard classical usage, these do not necessarily amount to enough to conclude that this is not Sophocles' own closure.

MORE ABOUT **OXFORD WORLD'S CLASSICS**

The Oxford World's Classics Website

www.worldsclassics.co.uk

- Browse the full range of Oxford World's Classics online
- Sign up for our monthly e-alert to receive information on new titles
- Read extracts from the Introductions
- Listen to our editors and translators talk about the world's greatest literature with our Oxford World's Classics audio guides
- Join the conversation, follow us on Twitter at OWC_Oxford
- Teachers and lecturers can order inspection copies quickly and simply via our website

www.worldsclassics.co.uk

MORE ABOUT **OXFORD WORLD'S CLASSICS**

American Literature

British and Irish Literature

Children's Literature

Classics and Ancient Literature

Colonial Literature

Eastern Literature

European Literature

Gothic Literature

History

Medieval Literature

Oxford English Drama

Philosophy

Poetry

Politics

Religion

The Oxford Shakespeare

A SELECTION OF **OXFORD WORLD'S CLASSICS**

Niccolò Machiavelli	The Prince
Thomas Malthus	An Essay on the Principle of Population
Karl Marx	Capital The Communist Manifesto
J. S. Mill	On Liberty and Other Essays Principles of Political Economy and Chapters on Socialism
Friedrich Nietzsche	Beyond Good and Evil The Birth of Tragedy On the Genealogy of Morals Thus Spoke Zarathustra Twilight of the Idols
Thomas Paine	Rights of Man, Common Sense, and Other Political Writings
Jean-Jacques Rousseau	The Social Contract Discourse on the Origin of Inequality
Arthur Schopenhauer	The Two Fundamental Problems of Ethics
Adam Smith	An Inquiry into the Nature and Causes of the Wealth of Nations
Mary Wollstonecraft	A Vindication of the Rights of Woman